UNDERSTANDING BIBLE TEACHING

Jesus as Man

H L Ellison BA, BD

Scripture Union

47 Marylebone Lane, London W1 6AX

Wm. B. Eerdmans

225 Jefferson Avenue, Grand Rapids, Michigan

First published 1973
First published in this form 1978

ISBN 0 85421 708 5 (Scripture Union)
ISBN 0 8028 1764 5 (Wm. B. Eerdmans)

Printed in Great Britain at the Benham Press
by William Clowes & Sons Limited, Colchester and Beccles

General Introduction

There are many commentaries on the Biblical text and there are many systematic studies of Christian doctrine, but these studies are unique in that they comment on selected passages relating to the major teachings of the Bible. The comments are designed to bring out the doctrinal implications rather than to be a detailed verse by verse exposition, but writers have always attempted to work on the basis of sound exegetical principles. They have also aimed to write with a certain devotional warmth, and to demonstrate the contemporary relevance of the teaching.

These studies were originally designed as a daily Bible reading aid and formed part of Scripture Union's Bible Characters and Doctrines series. They can, of course, still be used in this way but experience has shown that they have a much wider use. They have a continued usefulness as a summary and exposition of Biblical teaching arranged thematically, and will serve as a guide to the major passages relating to a particular doctrine.

Writers have normally based their notes on the RSV text but readers will probably find that most modern versions are equally suitable. Many, too, have found them to be an excellent basis for group Bible study. Here the questions and themes for further study and discussion will prove particularly useful—although many individuals will also find them stimulating and refreshing.

ONE

Jesus' Birth and Childhood

1 : The Preparation

Luke 1.5–25

God's ability to create from nothing, to make light shine out of darkness, mesmerizes some, so they find no room for the slow and unerring unfolding of His plans. Jesus was born when 'the time had fully come' (Gal. **4**.4); if He came to His own home (John **1**.11), i.e. the world, we should remember that He had both made it and controlled its development from the first, and above all, from the time of Abraham.

Here we are introduced to two products of the preparation, 'righteous . . . blameless', yet men privately pointed the finger of scorn at them, for they were childless; both being over sixty, all hope had gone. Yet another thing seemed to indicate Zechariah's being under Divine displeasure. All priestly service was fixed by lot; the burning of incense was considered so supreme that no one was chosen more than once in his life. Though he was one of the oldest functioning priests this lot had never fallen on Zechariah. Now the one day brought honour and promise, the former so that the latter might more easily be believed. Zechariah knew that the one standing by the altar (11) must be an angel, not because of his form, which was human, but because only an officiating priest could enter the Temple. For Gabriel see Dan. **8**.16; **9**.21.

Gabriel's message rose to a climax: your prayer is heard, a son John (which means 'Yahweh is gracious'), great, i.e. a prophet, a life-long Nazirite like Samuel, from the first under God's control, the bringer of reformation in an evil age, the fulfiller of Malachi's closing promise (**4**.5 f.) in its spiritual meaning ('in the spirit and power of Elijah'). It contained, however, an interesting change; 'the hearts of children to their fathers' becomes 'the disobedient to the wisdom of the just'. The generation gap has always existed, and it is the duty of parents, not to complain about it, but to try to understand and bridge it. On the other hand, when the children are touched by the Spirit of God, they must recognize that it is their godly parents who are correct.

Asking for a sign (18) may show faith or doubt; Zechariah doubted and so was punished. The people wondered at his delay, for entry into the Temple was considered dangerous and was kept as short as possible. They realized he had seen a vision, when he could give only the gestures of the Aaronic blessing but not the words.

2 : The Chosen Vessel

Luke 1.26–56

Of Mary's background we know nothing beyond the fact that she was descended from David. The universal Jewish custom of the time tells us that she was between twelve and twelve and a half when she was engaged, i.e. legally became Joseph's wife; she must have been under fourteen when Gabriel came to her, for that was the maximum age at which a marriage was consummated. Since Mary did not know that he was an angel, and it was bad form to speak to a strange woman, she was greatly troubled. Gabriel's message contains overtones of Isa. **7**.14; 2 Sam. **7**.14; Isa. **9**.7; Dan. **7**.14. Mary realized that this was not a promise about a child she might have by Joseph (34) but of one to be conceived almost immediately.

Gabriel told her this would be the work of the Holy Spirit (35). We would do well to be satisfied with this and not to seek for purely human explanations of the Virgin Birth and of the breaking of the entail of original sin. 'The child will be called holy' means he would belong entirely to God; 'Son of God' before Jesus' resurrection meant for a Jew the perfect revealer of God's character and will. In v. 37, 'for God's promises can never fail' (NEB, Phillips), is preferable. A godly Jewess did not need to be reminded of God's omnipotence; what was important for her was that the ancient promises were going into effect. 'I am the handmaid of the Lord' (38) means 'I am the Lord's slave'.

Mary's poem of thanksgiving should be compared with Hannah's (1 Sam. **2**.1–10), on which it is obviously based. Both celebrated God's reversal of man's standards and values. A concept of Christianity that makes it a religion of the *status quo* has completely missed its nature, cf. 1 Cor. **1**.26–31. Something of Mary's sweet humility is seen in her leaving

Elizabeth just before John's birth; she did not wish to deflect attention from her.

It is a great pity that the undue honour given Mary in certain circles, which has led to the attribution of sinlessness, a mediating role and worship, has caused others to give her too little. Though later Mary showed that she did not adequately understand the Son God had given her, yet in her humble acceptance of God's overwhelming will for her she is an object lesson for all.

3 : Joseph

Matthew 1.1–25 (Luke 3.23–38)

The main purpose of the genealogy is probably less to prove Jesus' legal claim to the Davidic throne, and more to show that He was not merely a revealer of divine truth but far more the climax of a divinely guided historical process. Luke gives His genealogy (3.23–38), which is also of Joseph, cf. NBD, p. 459, after the Baptism, so as to set Jesus' work as man in its human setting and to show Him as the second Adam. There can be little doubt that Jechoniah (Jehoiachin) in v. 11 is a scribal error for Johoiakim, which goes back to the Hebrew original. The device of breaking up the genealogy into three groups of fourteen names stresses the natural divisions of the history, gives an aid to memory, and stamps the name of David on each, for the value of the letters of his name in Hebrew adds up to fourteen.

Preferable in v. 18 is 'This is the story of the birth of the Messiah' (NEB, RSV mg.). Joseph is not called husband (19) in anticipation; their engagement made them a married couple —hence the need for a divorce, if they were to part. Joseph, by his acceptance of Mary and her child, made Jesus his legal son. Jesus (Heb. Yeshua) was the then accepted abbreviation of Joshua (Heb. *Yehoshua*) meaning Yahweh is Salvation, and was at the time a very common name. We constantly demand the new; God takes the old and fills it with a new meaning.

In Isa. 7.14 the RSV, NEB, Phillips, Knox, Jer.B. translate young woman or maiden, for the Hebrew word means an unmarried girl of marriageable age, whose virginity is taken for granted—hence the Greek, 'virgin', as quoted by Matthew. This prophecy, like numerous others, had a double fulfilment

By the time a girl, on the eve of marriage when Isaiah spoke, bore her first child, the danger threatening Jerusalem would have apparently passed; thrilled by the fact, his parents would call him Immanuel. Isaiah's further words show that the deliverance would be only apparent, and that the reality would come only after judgement, cf. Isa. **7**.17; **9**.2; **11**.1. Even had he used the technical word for virgin, its full implications would have become apparent only in the fulfilment. Though Jesus was Immanuel in the full sense, this could be grasped and enjoyed fully only after He was experienced as Saviour, so Jesus was the name given Him.

4 : The Nativity

Luke 2.1–20

In re-reading this most familiar of stories we must make an effort to rid ourselves of the pagan and sentimental accretions of popular tradition. All Israel did not go off to the cities of their most distant ancestors; Joseph, as the legal heir to the Davidic throne (Matt. **1**.1–16), had for obvious reasons kept his legal domicile in Bethlehem. There is no suggestion that they went there in winter and still less that Jesus was born on the night they arrived; if anything, v. 6 means the exact opposite. The word rendered 'inn' (except NEB) is elsewhere (**22**.11; Mark **14**.14) a guest room and should be so understood here. Owing to its nearness to Jerusalem it is improbable that Bethlehem had an inn at the time. The manger means no more than the portable wooden trough used for feeding the animals when they were admitted to the lower level of a house. The ox and ass of earlier Christian art—now multiplied to a whole farmyard!—were taken from Isa. **1**. 3 and were intended merely as a symbolic linking with Old Testament prophecy. The 'swaddling clothes' (7, 12) stress the normality of the baby. While there may be poverty in the picture, it is not abnormal; such could have been the surroundings of most new-born babies in Palestine.

It is often stressed that the sheep pastured in the fields of Bethlehem were destined for Temple sacrifices, and therefore their shepherds were chosen for pious reputation. This is doubtless true but should not be stressed. Theophilus (**1**.3) could not have known this; had Luke laid any stress on it, he would have explained it. Rather, the revelation of David's 'greater Son' was given to those who followed David's profession. However beautiful and true the AV rendering of the song of the heavenly host (14), the manuscript evidence is overwhelmingly in favour of the RV, RSV, NEB; the last renders well, '. . .for men on whom His favour rests'.

The shepherds' story created wonder among those who heard it (18). 'Wonder'—this looks forward to the ultimate rejection of Christ. The union of heaven's glory and absolute human normality is something that men feel to be irreconcilable. So they either reject or distort the balance. The popular distortion of the Christmas story can be particularly disastrous in the effect it has on young children, as it makes it seem like a fairy story.

5 : Earliest Infancy

Luke 2.21–39

Today circumcision is regarded by the average Jew mainly as a national sign, and by many non-Jews as a hygienic measure, but in New Testament times it was above all an indication that the child was under an obligation to keep the Law, cf. Gal. 4.4; hence the question of Gentile Christians' keeping the Law could be summed up by the demand for their circumcision. Part of Jesus' obedience was His acceptance of the conditions under which He was born. In the rare cases where we find Him stepping outside these limitations, it was for the good of others, and He normally justified His action by an appeal to Scripture.

The RSV and NEB follow older manuscripts in v. 22 in contrast to the AV. The latter conforms to the language of Lev. 12.1–5. By saying 'their purification' Luke was expressing the obvious fact that if the mother needed purification so did the child. He is not implying that Jesus needed it; it is his way of expressing Paul's phrase, 'sending His own Son in the likeness of sinful flesh' (Rom. 8.3). It is in Christ's resurrection that we have the assurance of His perfect sinlessness and deity (Rom. 1.4).

Simeon's hymn is based throughout on Old Testament Scripture, especially Isaiah. For 'a light for revelation to the Gentiles', cf. Isa. 42.6; 49.6 and to some extent 60.3. Jesus is

Israel (Isa. **49**.3), and so its glory, for He is everything that Israel should have been and was not, that Israel wished to be and yet could not be. Jesus is the perfect revelation of God to the world and the perfect justification of God's election of Israel.

The only way in which v. 39 can reasonably be reconciled with the story in Matt. **2** is first of all to separate the latter from Luke's nativity story by a period of time, as is indeed suggested by Herod's killing of the boys up to two years of age. It may thus be understood that after the presentation in the Temple Joseph and Mary returned to Nazareth (39) and sold up there. Then they returned to Bethlehem. Joseph evidently considered that the promised Messiah should not only be born but also brought up in David's city. Luke had no interest in mentioning the second Bethlehem visit, for, unlike Matthew, he does not stress Jesus as the Messianic king but as the representative man, cf. his tracing of His genealogy back to Adam.

6 : The Coming of the Magi

Matthew 2.1–23

In this story too we must strip away modern sentimental accretions. We are not told how many astrologers (NEB, Phillips) there were—earlier Christian tradition suggested up to twelve—and they were certainly not kings. Presumably the rising of the star (NEB, Jer.B.) was at the time of Jesus' birth, so their arrival must have been at least some months later, cf. v. 16. There is no suggestion that they were led by the star, cf. v. 9. Matthew does not explain how the astrologers came to link the star with the expected king of the Jews—he does not even mention Num. **24**.17—what its nature was, or how it could at the last move before them. The important thing is that none of the priests and scribes (4) had the least interest in following up the matter; that was left to Gentiles, thus foreshadowing the ultimate outcome. The NEB and Phillips are very much better in vs. 2, 8, 11 with 'to pay him homage'. There is no suggestion that they recognized Jesus' deity.

'Gold, frankincense and myrrh' are very often expounded allegorically, but unless we assume that the astrologers had been given a special revelation, it is hardly wise to attribute knowledge to them unshared by their Jewish contemporaries. Perhaps we should rather see God's providing: gold for the cost of the expensive journey to Egypt; frankincense and myrrh, easy to transport but very valuable in Egypt, where they were in great demand for embalming, and so covering costs until Joseph could find work.

When Matthew applied Hos. **11**.1 (15) and Jer. **31**.15 (17, 18) to Jesus, he was implying that He was the fulfilment and personification of Israel. In some way He had to recapitulate Israel's history, the hidden years in Nazareth paralleling the wilderness wanderings. Rachel's sorrow was due to sin and a foreign king. Now these were combined in a king (Herod) with no claim to the throne. In addition, Jer. **31**.15 stands in close connection with the promise of the new covenant (Jer. **31**.31–34). So, too, the fulfilment of the promise was ushered in by suffering. Nazareth (23) is not mentioned in the Old Testament, but Nazarene (*notzri*) is reminiscent of 'shoot' (*netzer*) in Isa. **11**.1. In addition, the low status of Nazareth (John **1**.46) corresponds to that of the Suffering Servant.

7 : The Boy Jesus

Luke 2.40–52

Luke, stressing Jesus' role as representative man, points out that His development was that of a normal child and adolescent (40, 52). The stress was needed, for perverse natural piety was to delight in portraying Him as 'wielding the power of the Godhead with a child's waywardness and petulance', to quote Salmon on the Gospel of St. Thomas, dating back in some form to about A.D. 200. We should never try to go behind the New Testament and infer what knowledge and powers Jesus possessed before He began His ministry.

A Jewish boy, then as now, reached his religious majority at thirteen. Normally one began to initiate him into his religious responsibilities a year earlier, which shows why Jesus was twelve, when first taken to Jerusalem (42). Public teaching in the Temple (46) took place only on Sabbaths and feast-days. The feast had not finished when Jesus was found, so we infer that because of poverty Joseph and Mary started their return journey on the third day of Passover, when travel was again permitted and the main obligations of the feast had been fulfilled. An important part in Rabbinic teaching was played by listeners' questions; normally these were answered by questions designed to draw out the answer from the questioner. Hence we have a picture, not of Jesus teaching the rabbis, but a Boy of twelve asking questions not expected from that age, and when questioned in return showing knowledge (in the context, of a religious nature) far beyond what was expected.

The AV and Jer.B. in v. 49 subtly suggest that Jesus had misunderstood His Father's will. In fact, He was telling Mary that there had been no need to search; it was obvious that He would be in the Temple. Possibly Mary had used the opportunity of this visit to reveal the secret of His birth to Him.

In v. 52 we have a reminiscence of 1 Sam. **2**.26; Prov. **3**.4. The wisdom is that which comes from experience, from which most are so unwilling to learn. One could easily build too much on 'in favour with God'. Ponder Heb. **2**.10, 18; **5**.7–9, for these passages will have had their main fulfilment in the years in Nazareth. Remember, too, that in spite of the modern cult of youth, it has little value except as a foreshadowing of what maturity may bring.

Questions and themes for study and discussion on Studies 1-7

1. Is it ever right to ask for a sign? If so, when?
2. Compare and contrast the experience of Mary and Hannah.
3. Why are there so many genealogies in Scripture?
4. What makes men want to embroider the Nativity narrative and other Bible stories?
5. Why do you think Simeon was kept alive to see the Christ when others did not have this privilege?
6. In what ways can Jesus be described as 'the fulfilment and personification of Israel'?
7. What may modern parents learn from the story of our Lord's first Passover?

TWO

The Opening of Jesus' Ministry

8 : John's Ministry

Luke 3.1–20 (Matt. **3**.1–12; Mark **1**.1–8; John **1**.19–28)

In popular thought little place is found for John's ministry in spite of a statement like Luke **7**.24–28. Jesus is pictured as sweeping at least the common people off their feet by His eloquence and love, the simplicity of His teaching and His miracles. In at least four features John was responsible for an all-important preparation.

1. John was a 'freak', Jesus was a normal man (Luke **7**.33 f). Repeatedly the abnormal man standing on the fringe of society has been needed to stir the conscience and imagination of those tied to routine before another could change society from within. The best Old Testament example is Elijah and his successor Elisha. To go out into the wilderness is not normally God's way of salvation, but until some do the masses will not be stirred to seek the narrow gate that leads to life (Matt. **7**.13 f).

2. At the time there was a deep and burning hope of the Messianic deliverer, cf. Luke **2**.25, 38; John **1**.19–21, but it was, as is the Second Coming today, all too often a subject of discussion and speculation. John brought it to focus and made it a reality. We must not forget that what led His contemporaries to accept or reject Jesus was normally their decision whether He was or was not one whom they could accept as Messiah.

3. Though it was generally accepted that the Messiah's coming was linked with religious and moral demands, these were generally taken to be superficial and marginal. We see some of them reflected in the New Testament purity of race (8), observance of the ritual law, cf. the Sabbath controversies, fasting (Mark **2**.18–22), ritual washing (Mark **7**.1–8). The Zealots, fanatical nationalists, considered national liberation justified murder and other illegal acts; some preached what today is called a Socialist revolution. John stressed that the coming of the Kingdom of God (Matt. **3**.2) meant judge-

ment as well as blessing, the criterion being life not words.

4. At least two of Jesus' first disciples (John **1**.35) were first among John's, and John **1**.35–51 probably implies that all mentioned there had been first influenced by him.

It is important to remember that though John had withdrawn from society (Luke **1**.80), his demands were all to be carried out within society. Much of his teaching is reflected in 1 Cor **7**.24. Note that his 'socialism' (11) was based on giving, not taking. His baptism implied a completely new beginning.

9 : The Baptism and Temptation

Luke 3.21, 22; 4.1–13 (Matt. 3.13–4.11; Mark 1.9–13; John 1.24–34)

Though John and Jesus were cousins (Luke **1**.36), it is unlikely there had been many contacts. So John's unwillingness to baptize Him was probably due to prophetic insight rather than personal knowledge. Jesus' willingness to be baptized was part of His identification with sinners. In addition, as said on Luke **2**.22 (Study No. 5), it is the resurrection which is the Father's guarantee of His Son's sinlessness. In all four accounts the stress is on the descent of the Holy Spirit. We are to theorize on what it meant for God to face human difficulties and temptations. In the Gospels the stress is that Jesus was the perfect Man, who from His conception (Luke **1**.35) was kept holy by the Spirit, who also caused Him to triumph in temptation. We are asked to share in that power.

The Father's commendation (22) was, as the Greek makes clear, not merely His approval of the Baptism, but also and primarily His acceptance of His life up till then. Through the Septuagint it is also linked with Isa. **42**.1.

It would be truer to the meaning of the Greek and the spiritual significance of the story, if we spoke of testing rather than temptation, the older meaning of which was testing. Jesus was not being urged to do anything morally wrong, but simply to follow entirely natural impulses without reference to the Spirit's guidance. The first was to use spiritual powers for personal ends (3). Jesus used these powers to feed or heal, when the needs of others demanded it, but never as an advertisement. The quotation from Deut. **8**.3b implies that

God, the Giver of all, should decide how His gifts should be used. The second (5–7) was a call to compromise in recognition of the fact that Satan is the ruler of this world (John **14**.30; 1 John **5**.19). The NEB renders better with 'do homage'. But the recognition of other powers in this way is a denial of God's omnipotence. The third (9–11) suggested that God be forced to display His miraculous powers on His behalf. We fall into this temptation easily, thinking we glorify God by forcing Him to show His power. The power is there, but it must be used as God wishes. Matthew transposes the second and third, probably because he is stressing Jesus' role as King.

10 : The First Disciples

John 1.29–51

John said of Jesus. 'He must increase, but I must decrease' (John **3**.30) and allowed his conviction above all by passing on his disciples to Jesus (35–37). Though unprovable, it is probable that all six mentioned here had been influenced by John first. 'He first' (41) probably implies that the unnamed disciple, i.e. John, then found his brother James. Nathanael, cf. **21**.2, is probably Bartholomew, who is always paired with Philip in the Synoptic lists (Matt. **10**.3; Mark **3**.18; Luke **6**.14). Andrew's and Philip's words (41, 45) show that both Peter and Nathanael were deeply concerned with the coming Messiah promised by John. Our tendency is to press the younger Christian to committal in Christian work. Jesus permitted these six, and perhaps the others also, to get to know Him more closely before He called them to complete identification with Him, cf. Mark **1**.16–20. After all, the Spirit knows the right time better than we do.

It is clear that the whole section from v. 19 on comes after Jesus' temptation. It was given to John to see, even though he could hardly have known the details—these were probably given to the disciples after the resurrection—that Jesus by His rejection of Satan's suggestions had made the pathway of suffering and death inevitable, and hence was the Servant of Isa **53**. The AV and RV are correct in placing 'beareth' in the margin (29) alongside 'taketh away'; both are implied, cf. RSV mg. to 1 Pet. **2**.24.

We have here an array of titles given to Jesus: Lamb of God (29), Son of God (34, 49)—for the usage see comments on Luke **1**.35—Rabbi (38,49), i.e. Teacher, Messiah (41), King of Israel (49), yet clearly they come to a climax in Son of Man, the representative man and the coming world ruler (Dan. **7**.13). It is often stated that John, in contrast to the Synoptics, stresses the deity rather than the manhood of Jesus. In fact, all these titles are illuminated in various ways in this Gospel, but above all, the last, even though it is not used so often. The mystery John illumines is above all how God can be truly man. It is this mystery that creates the ladder linking God and man (51). It is not likely that we should lay any special stress on the angels. Jesus is the one and only true link by which man's needs ascend to God and God's blessings descend to man. The angels may bear the gifts but they are Jesus' servants, and through Him ours (Heb. **1**.14).

11 : The First Miracle

John 2.1–12

John records seven miracles by Jesus and uses the term 'sign' to designate them, though he indicates that there were many more (**20**.30). The limitation to seven and the use of 'sign' indicate that the stories chosen have a deeper purpose than the mere narration of the miraculous.

Certain details can easily be added to John's account. Mary's active participation behind the scenes suggests that one of the bridal pair was a relation. Possibly, Jesus and His disciples were invited at the last moment; this would explain the wine's running short and Mary's turning to Jesus; there is no evidence that she expected a miracle. Jesus' answer defies idiomatic translation. She is 'woman', cf. **19**.26, not 'Mother', for His actions were not to be swayed by special affection to her or the bridal couple. Then her approach to the problem was not His. He knew the need, but awaited His hour (4), i.e. the time appointed by the Father for Him to work, cf. **7**.3-10. It may be that having filled the six jars with water, the servants then drew more from the well (Westcott), or that only what was taken from the jars became wine (NBC); John's failure to make this clear shows how unimportant it was to him.

The various attempts at symbolic or allegoric interpretation have nothing to commend them. It is clear from v. 11 that John is writing of something that had an immediate effect on the disciples, not of deeper meanings which gradually came to them.

Temple may well be correct in seeing a picture of the change brought about by our first contact with Christ, 'a change like that from water to wine'. The coming of Christ may well bring distortions and needs to our lives. There is many a hard-pressed family which wonders how it can possibly meet the demands of Christ's work a home and abroad, demands on time as well as money, if it opens itself to His demands. Yet if He is welcomed—it may be at the moment when all human resources run out—from what is there Christ can provide the extra that is needed, an extra bringing joy in its train. What Jesus would not do for Himself in the wilderness He now did for those who had invited Him to share their joy. As for Himself, He foreshadowed the future by leaving home (12).

Questions and themes for study and discussion on Studies 8-11

1. John the Baptist has been called 'the neglected prophet'. Can you suggest reasons for this neglect?
2. It has been said that just as the cross and the resurrection throw light on each other, so also do our Lord's baptism and temptations. In what ways?
3. What was there about Jesus which was so attractive to the men who left all to follow Him?
4. How do we see the glory of Christ manifested in His first miracle?

THREE

The Early Judean Ministry

12 : The Cleansing of the Temple

John 2.13–22

Sacrificial animals had to pass the scrutiny of the sacrificing priest. Hence, even for those living near Jerusalem, there was a major advantage in having a market of guaranteed animals; for those from other countries it was a necessity. Such a market was held on the Mount of Olives. It is easy to understand that the temple-authorities saw the advantage of having it held more under their control. The court of the Gentiles was not officially part of the Temple, though regarded as having a greater degree of sanctity than the rest of Jerusalem.

There is little difference between the story of the cleansing of the Temple and that in Mark **11**.15–17, and it is widely maintained that there has been a misplacement, deliberate or accidental. The arguments used carry little conviction. The use of the court of the Gentiles as a cattle-market had such obvious advantages for the leading priests that a repetition was to be expected.

Jesus began His ministry by facing official Judaism in its citadel—note 'the Passover of the Jews' (13). In contrast to His second cleansing of the Temple, Jesus had come to Jerusalem as an unknown man, but by His actions and words ('My Father's house') He proclaimed His authority. He was asked to justify His claim (18), as He was more than once later, cf. Matt. **12**.38; **16**.1, because Moses had validated his mission by signs (Exod. **4**.1–9, 30). Had Jesus refused any sign, we could understand it, but a purely future one (19), cf. Matt. **12**.39, seems strange, until we remember that Moses had been given a future event as a sign (Exod. **3**.12). To an enslaved people, ground down by hard labour, God might graciously give signs of His favour and presence, but where men claim to know Him, cf. John **8**.33; **9**.40 f., God's signs must be linked with the exercise of faith and come as a confirmation of it—but see the next section.

There was an ambiguity in the sign which Jesus' disciples

grasped only later (22). Because He was the true Temple, uniquely indwelt by the Holy Spirit (John **3**.34), He was implicitly the One who would abolish this and any other earthly temple made with hands, cf. John **4**.21; 1 Cor. **3**.16; **6**.19; Eph. **2**.20–22; Rev. **21**.22. Jesus had not yet begun His normal ministry. He was presenting Himself to the religious leaders of the people for recognition, but there was 'no beauty that they should desire him'.

13 : Nicodemus

John 2.23–3.21

We do not know the signs Jesus did in Jerusalem (23)—presumably compassionate acts of healing—but they were not intended as answers to the challenge in v. 18. For lovers of the miraculous there comes the staggering statement that though 'many trusted on his name . . . Jesus did not trust himself to them' (23 f., Temple)—a play on words normally ignored. The sight of the miraculous may produce a counterfeit of true faith that deceives all but Christ.

Nicodemus came representing his fellow teachers—'we' (2) —'by night', the most suitable time for serious conversation. His opening words were a politely veiled invitation for a specimen of Jesus' teaching; they wanted to know whether they could invite Him to join them in teaching. Compliments may make life easier, but they are out of place where the issues of life and eternity are involved. Further, the greater a person's religious knowledge the less the value of generalized discussion. By mentioning the Kingdom of God Jesus turned Nicodemus' attention to John's preaching (Matt. **3**.1f); he may well have been one of the delegation of John **1**.19–24. So water (5) probably refers to John's baptism, or rather the repentance with which it was linked; the suggestion that it stands for Christian baptism or the Scriptures has nothing to commend it. Jesus' surprise (10) was because the mention of water and spirit should have reminded Nicodemus of Ezek. **36**.25–27. From vs. 11 f. we may infer that some of Jesus' disciples were present ('we') and also some of Nicodemus' ('you', plural), and such would have been normal Jewish practice. They had not understood or believed what Jesus had told them about things that happened 'on earth'

(12, NEB), hence it was pointless for Him to speak about the heavenly realities behind them. He could, for He had descended from heaven to be lifted up for man's salvation (13–15, cf. **12**.32). Jesus' use of 'Son of man' here (13) clearly refers to Dan. **7**.13. It is disputed whether 'who is in heaven' should be added to v. 13; if we do, it probably means 'whose home is in heaven' (NEB).

It is also disputed whether vs. 16–21 were said to Nicodemus (Phillips, NEB), or are a commentary by John (RSV). It is not important, for in either case they bring out the implications of vs. 14 f. Not all are covered by v. 18; some have had no possibility of belief because they have never heard. Perhaps we should say of them only that Christ died for them and in the judgement day will declare whether they would have believed had the possibility existed.

14 : The Forerunner Decreases

John 3.22–36

It may be that v. 24 merely corrects a false impression that could be created by Matt. **4**.12; Mark **1**.14; more probably it explains why Jesus' disciples, not Jesus, were baptizing (22, 26; **4**.1 f.). While His forerunner was still active, Jesus, though presenting Himself as the fulfiller of John's message, did nothing to detract from his activity. We saw that Jesus' first disciples had been linked with John; now they were continuing his work. This was not Christian baptism in the full sense.

It is immaterial whether we read 'a Jew' (RSV) or 'Jews' (AV, NEB) in v. 25. It seems that some tried to depreciate John's work by pointing to Jesus' greater popularity. The very fact that they disputed about purifying shows that the real points at issue had been forgotten or misunderstood. Standard Judaism was dominated by concepts of defilement and purification. This is no longer true, the destruction of the Temple —where purification was effected—having removed the possibility of it. They could not understand Christ's teaching on heart defilement (Mark **7**.1–23). Seeing defilement as something purely external, they could not understand the symbolism of John's baptism, not cleansing but a cutting off from the past, cf. 1 Pet. **3**.21 f.

It is difficult to say whether John fully realized what his

decreasing (30) involved. He had become so well known and popular that no slow elimination would have been adequate. His arrest by Herod and subsequent execution were a necessity and a measure of his greatness. We may be sure that John accepted this drastic decreasing without hesitation.

As with John 3.16–21, we cannot be sure whether we hear the evangelist's comments in vs. 31–36 or the voice of John the Baptist; the latter is more probable. In either case it explains why even the teaching ministry of John was inadequate compared to Jesus'. Some have taken 'yet no one receives his testimony' (32) as the evangelist's comment on the world situation at the time he wrote; this is improbable. We see from v. 32 that the statement should not be taken absolutely; rather it reinforces vs. 3, 5. Only the regenerate can really accept Jesus' teaching. 'It is not by measure that he gives the Spirit' (34) is a most important statement. On the basis of Phil. 2.7—'He emptied himself'—many claim that Jesus was ignorant of much and so liable to err. Though we know nothing precise of what the self-emptying involved, the Spirit 'without measure' is a guarantee of Jesus' infallibility.

15 : The Samaritan Woman

John 4.1–42

Having presented Himself to the leaders of Jewry, Jesus then did the same to the schismatic Samaritans. They were essentially the descendants of Ephraim and western Manasseh, with an admixture of foreign blood. Fundamentally orthodox, their chief aberrations were the rejection of all Old Testament books except the Pentateuch, and of Zion as God's choice for worship, claiming Mt. Gerizim (20) instead. Since their leaders were religiously illegitimate Jesus presented Himself obliquely through a woman—one of little repute at that. It is highly probable that Philip's successful ministry (Acts 8.5–8) in a city of Samaria (RSV, NEB, Jer.B.) was the sequel to what we read here.

Westcott points out that the verb translated 'left' (3) really means to leave something to itself. The report that Jesus was making more disciples than John (1) merely placed Him on the same general level and showed that the spiritual leaders had not recognized His true role. The only physical compulsion to pass through Samaria (4) was pressure of time and this seems denied by v. 40; hence it was more likely to be spiritual.

The woman, like many others, tried to hide her inner dissatisfaction by stress on non-essentials. It was less the sin and more the emptiness in her life that had been touched by Jesus. True, she tried to dodge the issue by raising the principal point of controversy between Jew and Samaritan (20), but, as with Thomas after the resurrection (John **20**.24 f.), it was probably because she felt the possibility being held out to her too good to be true.

In a day when it is being increasingly suggested that the man in the street cannot grasp Christian theology it is worth stressing that Jesus expected this woman to understand a principle of God's nature, and hence of worship, which many theologians have failed to grasp. God, being spirit, does not need the material, however much He may use it for man's benefit (23 f).

We must beware of a Docetic Christ, i.e. one where manhood and its needs were merely an outward appearance. Just as He was genuinely hungry after His fast (Luke **4**.2), so He was genuinely tired after a long tramp (6). The joy, however, of doing His Father's work (34) removed the natural pangs of hunger (32).

Questions and themes for study and discussion on Studies 12-15

1. What implications for Christian worship are there in the fact that our Lord is Himself the true Temple of God?
2. To what extent may the Christian come to share his Lord's discernment of what is in men?
3. Why did Jesus need a forerunner?
4. What can the Christian personal worker learn from the stories of Nicodemus and the Samaritan woman?

FOUR

The Galilean Ministry (1)

16 : The Healing of the Official's Son

John 4.43–54

There is deep Divine irony in v. 44. Though it is not expressly stated, we can be sure that one of the main reasons for Jesus' rejection in Judea was the belief that He was a Galilean, cf. **7**.52. Nazareth rejected Him (Luke **4**.16–30) because it thought it knew all about Him; Judea because it did not know enough. The Galileans' enthusiasm (45) probably came in the first place from local pride. It is worth noting how seldom Christian artists really portray Jesus as a Jew.

It is often suggested that the story of the court official's son is merely a variant of that of the centurion's servant (Matt. **8**.5–13; Luke **7**.1–10) but there is no vestige of evidence for the theory. There is no reason for thinking the official was a Gentile, but the centurion probably knew him and so derived his confidence in Jesus. A useful study is Jesus' hard sayings; with v. 48 we might compare Matt. **15**.26; **17**.17; Mark **3**.33–35; **10**.18; Luke **9**.57–62. We have to know a person very well before we venture to interpret his words; Jesus understood what people meant, not what they seemed to say, cf. John **2**.25.

The official thought that Jesus was one of those inexplicable persons possessed of para-normal powers divorced from any obvious moral purpose, a miracle worker of the type Satan had tempted Jesus to be (Luke **4**.9–11). Jesus told him He had come to create faith, not work miracles, which do not necessarily produce true faith. Perhaps he had formerly been like Naaman (2 Kings **5**.11); now he threw himself on Jesus' mercy and believed the simple word spoken (49 f.). Something of the greatness of his faith may be judged by the fact that it is about twenty miles as the crow flies from Cana to Capernaum.

It can hardly be chance that the first two signs given us by John are among the least comprehensible of Jesus' miracles. Even where we have no wish to deny the miraculous, we are often glad to grasp at semi-scientific explanations. These two warn us that we gain little by such efforts. John, giving the seventh sign, makes it clear that Jesus was acting as God's representative, that it was the Father acting at His request (**11**.41 f.). We by our prayers act on others for their good at any distance. Jesus, the perfect Man of prayer, received the perfect answer.

17 : The Call of the King

Mark 1.14–20 (Matt. 4.18–22; Luke 5.1–11)

John had finished his forerunner's work; there remained only for him to seal it by suffering and death. Jesus could now begin His full activity. In one way His message was the same as John's; both said, 'The kingdom of God is at hand' (15, Matt. 3.2), or better, 'The kingdom of God has arrived' (Phillips), for it had come in the person of the King. But Jesus added 'the gospel'. It was not given to John fully to grasp how the Judge could also be the Reconciler. The gospel was essentially Jesus Himself; He displayed by His actions God's good will to men, and for those with eyes to see He showed that He was the King.

A king without subjects is a contradiction in terms, and so in Mark we are early introduced to His full-time disciples. All four had first come to Him through the Baptist, directly or indirectly. Then, however, it was an introduction; now came the kingly call to committal. The natural inference from the story of the Temple tax (Matt. **17**.24–27) is that only Jesus and Peter were liable to the tax, a liability that began at twenty. This is supported by consistent Church tradition that Peter was the oldest of the disciples, and he is the only one of them whose wife is mentioned in the Gospels (Mark **1**.30).

In the great spiritual changes that have influenced the Church the original insights have, more often than not, come from older men, but they have normally been carried through by younger men. Utter loyalty to Christ does not by itself create the flexibility of mind needed for new concepts. Jesus was also respecting the claims of family life in calling mainly unmarried men to abandon their normal responsibilities. Taken in a wider setting John **2**.12 suggests that Jesus arranged for His mother and brothers before beginning His full ministry, cf. John **19**.26 f. Far too many young people today create responsibilities for themselves before they know Christ's purpose for their lives. If Jesus did not marry for our sakes, we can defer marriage a little for His.

Those who admire acting on the spur of the moment should ponder the fact that Peter was able to fall back on his boat and nets when he needed them (John **21**.3). In addition, it should be obvious that James and John had told their parents of their earlier experiences with Jesus. There is no reason for thinking that Zebedee was not in favour of their following Jesus' call, cf. Matt. **20**.20.

18 : The Return to Nazareth

Luke 4.14–30 (Matt. **13**.53–58; Mark **6**.1–6)

Though its outcome was similar, the visit described in Matthew and Mark must be clearly distinguished from the earlier one told us by Luke. Here we find that Jesus revisited Nazareth quite early during His ministry; we may even infer that He had not yet called His disciples, cf. Luke **5**.1–11. The fact that He had recently moved to Capernaum (John **2**.12) may well have created a background of ill will, cf. v. 23. In addition, in a society where social position was largely fixed by land-ownership, the landless carpenter was looked down on. Jesus had not yet become famous, though for Nazareth He was a seven-days' wonder. They offered Him the honour of the reading of the prophetic portion, which followed that of the Law (there was no fixed lectionary at the time). This honour included the right of preaching the sermon, which was done sitting down as a mark of the teacher's authority.

Luke gives us only the vital part of the reading and the central thought of the sermon (21), which must have been of considerable length and conforming to the pattern of Mark **1**.14 f. The reaction was, 'What a wonderful sermon to come from *him*!' (22). Jesus told them that because they were not prepared to accept Him as God's prophet, i.e. spokesman, cf. Exod. **7**.1 f., they could not reap the benefit of having a prophet in their midst. They showed their incomprehension by treating Him as a blasphemer—throwing over the edge of the hill was the first step in stoning. Once out of the town Jesus just 'walked straight through them all' (NEB), as they were suddenly struck by the full impact of His character, cf. John **8**.59; **10**.39; **18**.6.

On His later visit Jesus came with His disciples (Mark **6**.1) and gave some considerable teaching (the force of the Greek in Matt. **13**.54). Fancied familiarity still bred contempt, but now there was no attempt to vent their anger on Him. The result, however, was the same. They excluded themselves from experiencing the power of God in their midst. These two incidents show how completely Jesus had veiled His powers and glory during the long years in Nazareth, while He was waiting for His Father's call. On the other hand, it is most likely that James' description of true religion (**1**. 27) was based on his memories of his older brother's life during that time.

19 : The Authority of Jesus

Mark 1.21–42 (Matt. 8.1–4, 14–17; Luke 4.31–44)

We are here introduced to the main bone of contention between Jesus and the Pharisees. Orthodox Jewish teachers have always disclaimed any authority beyond that inherent in the Law and the consensus of their fellow teachers. The 'ordination' of a rabbi is no more than the recognition by a number of recognized rabbis that he has sufficient knowledge of Law and tradition to expound them. Examples of Jesus' authority in teaching are found both in a passage like Matt. **5**.17–48 and in His general attitude. This involved the rejection of the scribes and Pharisees as authorities—though not necessarily of their teaching, cf. Matt. **23**.2 f.—and so they rejected Jesus.

His authority in matters spiritual was confirmed by His authority over spirit beings (23–26). There follows His authority in the realm of creation. In the story of Peter's mother-in-law we find a touch that constantly recurs and which for a doctor is far more puzzling than the miracles themselves. Growing stress is laid today on the 'psychosomatic' nature of much illness, and so the possibility of spiritual healing is increasingly accepted. This cannot explain that none of the debilitating effects of a high fever was seen (31); this shows the power of the Creator.

The crowds, without realizing the deeper implications of Jesus' presence, saw that there was the golden opportunity for healing (32 f.). They waited until sunset so as not to profane the Sabbath. Matt. **8**.17 makes clear that Jesus did not heal simply by a word of power. On the cross He identified Himself with human sin to destroy it; in *life* He identified Himself with human sickness to destroy it. We infer from vs. 38 f. that what happened in Capernaum was typical of events elsewhere.

Leprosy, not necessarily identical with the disease so called today, but rarely curable (Lev. **14**.2), was chosen by God as a picture of human sin in the defilement it caused. Jesus not only healed, but by touching the leper demonstrated that He could not be contaminated by his impurity. The leper's presenting himself to the priest would be not merely a proof of his healing, but also that God had sent a Healer. We sometimes stress the guilt of sin to the exclusion of its defilement, which is just as evil; it is particularly stressed in Ezekiel and Hebrews. Jesus has dealt equally with both.

20 : Authority to Forgive

Mark 2.1–17 (Matt. 9.1–13; Luke 5.17–32)

From leprosy, the outward picture of sin, Mark passes to sin itself. Some details of the story are difficult to fill in. If the RV mg., RSV, NEB are correct in rendering 'at home' (1), the house cannot have been the larger building postulated by some commentaries but a one-roomed structure, with a flat, earthen roof, supported by matting resting on cross-beams. To dig a hole through did not imperil those underneath, and the damage could be easily repaired. No indication is given of the paralytic's sin, nor why his friends had such a sense of urgency.

'My boy'—'son' is too formal—'your sins are at this moment forgiven,' said Jesus, thereby making it clear that it was their faith (5) that had led to this. Clearly enough the paralytic was, at least for the moment, satisfied by the unexpected words. But the theologians present (the scribes, v. 6) immediately thought, 'Unscriptural! blasphemy!' Jesus did not question their unimpeachable theology, but proclaimed Himself 'Son of man', clearly looking to Dan. 7.13, where 'one like unto a son of man' is given authority on earth as God's representative. Jesus claimed that this authority covered the forgiveness of sins. Obviously it is equally easy to say,

'Your sins are forgiven' and 'Rise'; equally obviously for those present both would have been equally ineffective. Jesus' ability to cure the paralytic with a word was proof to those willing to believe that the same word of power could cure the sin that lay behind the disease. Clearly, however, the crowd was more impressed by the healing than by the possibility of sins forgiven.

It is not chance that all three Synoptics, with all their willingness to change order, put the call of Levi (Matthew) immediately after the healing of the paralytic. Once one has compromised oneself, as Matthew had, by getting into despised and wrong surroundings, it is often as hard to free oneself as it was for the paralytic to walk. Indubitably Matthew had heard Jesus more than once, and his longing for something better had been easy to read. We must not picture him leaving money and accounts lying about to follow Jesus. He will have been sitting with other collectors near the custom house—the force of the Greek preposition—waiting to go on duty, or having just finished it. The Pharisees were of course correct; 'Bad company corrupts good morals' (1 Cor. **15**.33). But just as a doctor is not restrained by fear of infection, when called to a sick man's side, so the Christian will allow the Spirit to lead him into company he would not normally dare to enter.

21 : Man's Law and God's Activity

Mark 2.18–3.6 (Matt. **9**.14–17; **12**.1–14; Luke **5**.33–**6**.11)

Fasts among the Jews could be regular statutory ones, private ones due to special grief, and regular private fasts, cf. Luke **18**.12, mainly because of the prevalence of public sin. The last gives the background of v. 18. Rabbinic law forbade fasting among those taking part in a wedding, which could not be held on a statutory fast day. Jesus' answer was the more apposite because the Messianic period was compared to a wedding, cf. Rev. **19**.7–9. Many take 'they will fast in that day' as a command for Christian fasting—something permissible—but the parables of the patch and the wine-skins make this improbable. Christianity is something so new that Old Testament yardsticks are irrelevant for measuring conduct.

The Pharisees objected to the action of Jesus' disciples—

note that Jesus did not do it—because they were technically reaping and threshing (Luke **6**.1) on the Sabbath. In fact, there was here by Rabbinic tradition a clash of duties, for in honour of the Sabbath a man should avoid hunger (Matt. **12**.1). That explains Jesus' reference to David's action and to the priests' service in the Temple on the Sabbath (Matt. **12**.5). Clashes of principle occur more often than we sometimes allow. Jesus then laid down two principles. The Sabbath is God's gift to man, and the Son of man, as God's representative, is the One who shows how the Sabbath is to be used. Since the Pharisees considered that legal interpretations were to be made by the majority in the light of the past, this was a denial of their authority.

The Rabbinic interpretation and development of the Law were normally far more sensible than is generally granted. They laid down that a doctor should not be disturbed on the Sabbath unless life was at risk—a rule many doctors would welcome today. The man (1) was not in pain and had doubtless grown accustomed to his disability. This made him an excellent test case. Jesus turned the point by introducing the antithesis of 'good' and 'harm', or 'save life' and 'kill'. Where we can affirm the former, we are in the realm of Heb. **4**.10. Jesus was entitled to deal with the man, because He knew He could do good and save life.

Hatred creates strange bedfellows. The Pharisees loathed the Herodians even more than the Sadducees, but their greater rejection of Jesus brought them together. The Herodians knew that Jesus' principles meant the rejection of Herodian ideals.

Questions and themes for study and discussion on Studies 16-21

1. What differentiates great faith from weak faith?
2. Jesus called His men *in* their own terms ('fishers of men') but *on* His. What can we learn from this in preaching the gospel to others?
3. Find biblical illustrations of the truth declared in Luke **4**.24.
4. What is spiritual authority?
5. Why did the scribes react so adversely to Jesus during His ministry?
6. Consider the Epistle to the Galatians as amplifying the thought of Mark **2**.21 f.

FIVE

The Galilean Ministry (2)

22 : The Choice of the Twelve

Luke 6.12–26 (Matt. **10**.2–6; Mark **3**.13–19)

From passages like Luke **8**.38; **9**.57–62 it is clear that to follow Jesus as a disciple there was needed either His call or permission. There came a time when the number became clumsy (17), too many being taken out of normal life, and they were an embarrassment when hospitality was offered. So Jesus chose an inner circle, their number symbolizing the tribes of Israel, 'to be with Him and to be sent out' (Mark **3**.14)—note the order. So important was it that they should be the right men that Jesus prayed all night. What a comment on our willingness to act on feelings or a 'hunch'. In spite of the prayer the Twelve included Judas. God's answers to prayers may achieve purposes we little guess. The suggestion that Jesus deliberately chose Judas, so that he might betray Him, is spiritually abominable and runs counter to all we find recorded about Judas.

In the choice of the Twelve, though they did not know it, Jesus was making the first preparations for the sequel to His death and resurrection. So the Father gave Him a foretaste of 'the great multitude which no man could number' (Rev. **7**.9) and of the blessing He was to bring (17–19).

The modern preacher is expected to keep records lest he preach the same sermon twice, at least under the same text. Jesus was a teacher and expected to repeat Himself; it mattered little whether He used the same or similar words. It shows lack of appreciation, therefore, to try to 'reconcile' vs. 20–49 with Matt. **5–7**, as though they were variant forms of the same address, even though the disciples are being addressed. Jesus was not commending physical need and suffering (20 f.), which could be produced by shiftlessness and sheer inability to cope, nor condemning possessions (24), which could be the fruit of hard work and economy; had it been so, He would hardly have accepted help from the well-to-do (Luke **8**.3). We must understand these beatitudes in the sense of Matt. 5.3–10—cf. vs. 22 f. with Matt. 5.11 f. At the same time, without self-assertion and self-confidence instead of trust in God, wealth was improbable; it was unlikely unless there was some sharp practice and extortion as well. Paul expressed Jesus' meaning in Phil. 4.11 f; we must accept much and little alike from God and use both to His glory.

23 : The Power of Love

Luke 6.27–49

The moment we take this passage, or similar ones in the Sermon on the Mount, as a new law, we find ourselves facing the impossible. Even if we force ourselves to obey, our hearts are disobeying. If, however, we love those mentioned, we shall find ourselves doing as Jesus said, because His love is at work in us. 'Abuse' (28) is too weak; better is 'mistreat' (TEV). The whole section is governed by love (27) interpreted by what we should like done to us (31). Effective non-resistance must spring from strength and be lovingly positive in operation, or it will only harm others.

While human love and generosity always tend to be our response to love and generosity, Divine love springs from the nature of God—theologically we call it grace—and pours itself out irrespective of response (32-36). It is called 'compassionate' (36, NEB); 'merciful' (AV, RSV) is an attribute of the judge, compassion of the Father-Creator. The concept goes back to a Hebrew word derived from 'womb', cf. Psa. 103.13 f. Our attitude towards others should be derived from our seeing our fellow men with the eyes of a common Father-Creator.

It is true that one who does not criticize is less likely to be criticized (37), but the impersonal passive construction in vs. 37 f, 'be judged, . . . condemned, . . . forgiven, . . . given', in the usage of the time, implied God as the agent. This does not imply the working out of one's own salvation, but that as one shows God's character through Christ's spirit, one has passed beyond judgement (Rom. 8.1), and there is no obstacle to the riches of God flowing through one.

Criticism being a denial of God's nature—the term 'criticism' is used because Jesus was not referring to lawful and necessary judicial functions—the one who indulges in it is blind and incapable of guiding aright (39). The highest the disciple can rise is to the level of his Teacher, and so we can never do aright what He did not do (41 f). The very fact of our trying is a measure of our falling short!

Sound doctrine and words are always better than false doctrine, but in themselves they do not make a true Christian. They can be based purely on the intellect, but a truly Christ-like life can be derived only from being in Christ, from completely accepting Him as Lord.

24 : Jesus' Tribute to John

Matthew 11.2–19 (Luke 7.18–35)

Even though John was 'a prophet . . . and more than a prophet' (9), he was a man of his time, influenced by contemporary ideas about the Messiah, so he was puzzled by Jesus' activity, probably more by what He did not do than by what He did. The question asked by his disciples was oblique (3), partly, perhaps, lest the title Messiah be overheard by Roman and Herodian spies, partly because there was deep reluctance to use it until the work of the Messiah had been accomplished. Jesus' answer was, 'The power of God is being demonstrated by Me, and I have introduced a new scale of values—*the poor* have good news preached to them.' It was left to John to draw his own conclusions (6), but Jesus would never conform to his or others' ideas of what He should do.

Jesus' tribute to John could be paraphrased, 'You did not go to see a time-server and politician'—it is said that politics is the art of the possible—'but one of God's spokesmen, and more than that, the forerunner of the Messiah. That places him higher than those that went before him, but the least of those who enter into the realization of the Messianic rule will stand even higher. His message has inflamed those who imagine that God's rule can be introduced by violence and other human methods. John's message continues and brings to a climax the consistent revelation of the Old Testament. Just as John did not satisfy men's ideas of Elijah's work, so the one whose way he prepared will not satisfy their conceptions of Messiah's work.' There are two forms of spiritual greatness. One is shown by the work to which men and women are called—how great the position of the Christian worker!—and this can be judged in this age. Then there is the greatness of character that will be made known at Christ's judgement seat and not until then.

Man unwilling to do God's will will always find an excuse. Asceticism may be praised until it makes uncomfortable demands. Equally normality, when it rises above man's experience of normality, finds itself rejected. True Christian living will vary between the patterns set by Jesus and John, but in any case will find itself criticized.

25 : The Penalty of Rejection

Matthew 11.20–30 (Luke 10.13–15, 21, 22)

We are in constant danger of forgetting Jesus' words in John **20**.29 (cf. 2 Cor. **5**.16), and of thinking how wonderful it would be if we could see Him and have fellowship with Him as had His first disciples. In fact, we might well have shared in the general disbelief. This section, the context of which is probably given in the Lukan setting, brings the matter to a head.

1. The better my religion the harder it may be to come to faith. The men of Galilee were better than those of Tyre, Sidon and Sodom, but just because they knew more about God, they found it harder to recognize God's representative.

2. Why then did God not show His signs there, or for that matter, in the great centres of heathen life, in the time of Jesus? Repentance is something very good, but it is insufficient in itself, cf. John **3**.5. In Matt. **12**.43–45 Jesus gives a picture of how the final result of repentance can be worse than the first. The Bible is full of pictures of repentance that led nowhere. Better the repentance that gets nowhere than no repentance, but repentance based purely on witnessing a miracle is not likely to have the spiritual basis that brings regeneration. It is not chance that in missionary history obvious miracles are normally confined to the early days of a new work; equally, in personal experience they are generally found at the beginnings of a person's contacts with Christ. In neither case does this apply to those signs of God's grace which are manifestations of a change of *character*.

3. Ultimately the knowledge of God is an act of grace (27). Jesus affirms that a true knowledge of God is only through

Him (John **14**. 9). We should always remember that the ultimate nature of the Son, the God-Man, defies human analogies and categories, and has never been adequately expressed in the standard creeds. Hence controversy on the subject is seldom profitable.

4. The rabbis laid great stress on a man's taking the yoke of the Law on himself, i.e. becoming subject to it. Jesus takes the place of the Law (29, cf. Gal. **3**.23–26). With a properly fitted yoke an animal can do far more work far more easily than without it. With His yoke—always made to measure!—we are doing His work. It is a great mistake to interpret 'labour . . . heavy laden' exclusively, or even primarily, of sin.

26 : The Parable of the Sower

Luke 8.4–21 (Matt. **13**.1–23; Mark **4**.1–20)

In New Testament days the sower went in front of the ploughman, who turned in the seed that had been broadcast. The sowing was immediately after the first autumn rains had softened the ground enough for the ploughshare. There was nothing to indicate what lay beneath the surface; not even where the ploughman would leave the right of way across the field. So the parable deals with the soil rather than the sower or the seed. No explanation is given as to why the soil differs. He who proclaims the gospel may not pick and choose, for he cannot know the nature of the soil where the seed is scattered.

Note that no blame is laid on the unproductive soils. There may be moral blameworthiness as a root cause, but it is not stressed. The path (5, 12) remained unreceptive because the ploughshare did not break it up—no question of a metalled road here! The soil above the rock was shallow (6, 13) because the ploughshare had never bitten deep; the limestone of Palestine, so long as it is soil-covered, is soft. The seeds of thorns (7, 14) were there because inadequate attempts at weeding had been made. How do we explain the varying response of the good soil (Matt. **13**.23)? Was it seed, soil, or the environment in the field? It needs little knowledge of life to tell us how many weaknesses are due primarily to heredity and environment, and that if we are not subject to certain weaknesses, it is entirely due to the grace of God. This links directly with our previous portion. However we choose to explain it, behind unbelief and belief there lies God's sovereign activity. Yet we have to balance this with the fact that Jesus Christ died for all (John **3**.16; Rom. **5**.18 f., 2 Cor. **5**.14 f.).

Jesus began His ministry in Jerusalem, but in the midst of pride of place and tradition there was little room for the seed to root. His first message and activity in Galilee was for everyone, but with growing rejection He increasingly turned from general proclamation to the nurturing of the seed in good soil. This, and similar parables, cf. Matt. **13**.1–52; Mark **4**.1–34, mark the turning point. Only to those who had was now to be given. Many exegetes fail to distinguish between Jesus' parabolic stories, which are simple to understand, and the nature parables, which cloak mysteries and unpopular truths.

27 : More Signs

Mark 4.35–5.20 (Matt. **8**.23–34; Luke **8**.22–39)

At the end of a long day of teaching Jesus was tired. So His disciples simply took Him across the lake in the boat from which He had been teaching (**4**.1), cf. NEB, Phillips, TEV (36). Jesus soon fell asleep—the mention of the cushion (38) is a sign of an eye-witness—and was not awakened by a heavy squall that swept over the lake. The frequently met opinion that He was interfering with the handling of the boat by being in the steersman's place is an example of over-refinement in exegesis. Were it meant, it would have been said; the parallels do not suggest it. In any case it would have been out of character. The disciples' attitude is interesting (38); they did not doubt Jesus' power, but His concern. For those in God's service there is no guarantee against drowning, literal or metaphorical, but if one is drowned, it is the working out of God's perfect will (Rom. **8**.28), and hence there are no grounds for fear (40). As with the miracles of healing, the effect was complete (39). Normally the falling of the wind, which could have been entirely natural, would be followed by a period of rough water.

Control over inanimate nature is of value only if it leads

to spiritual results. So the story of the storm-tossed lake is linked with that of the storm-tossed man. The impression created by a legion was, above all, of disciplined power, so the rendering 'Mob' (TEV) is particularly unfortunate. Just as Israel had succumbed to the might and discipline of Rome so this unfortunate individual had become the slave of the organised forces of evil. Nevertheless, faced with his Creator, his response was stronger than the spirits that had enslaved him. The man was probably a Jew, but since the district was predominantly Gentile, the pigs are not likely to have had Jewish owners. Many suggest that Jesus had no right to destroy the legitimate property of others, but if the drowning of the pigs was necessary for the man's rehabilitation, who will say the price was too high, the more so as God could have restored what was lost? The healed demoniac had to learn to live a normal life (19) before he became a preacher (20), something we are slow to remember. Why the unclean spirits were so anxious to enter the pigs (cf. Luke **8**.31) must with our inadequate knowledge remain a matter of conjecture.

28 : The Twelve and the Five Thousand

Luke 9.1–17 (Matt. **14**.1–21; Mark **6**.7–44; John **6**.1–14)

Luke narrates the sending out of the Twelve only briefly, because he gives the bulk of the instructions they received in connection with the sending out of the Seventy-two (**10**.1, NEB, RSV mg.), whose brief was similar. All three Synoptics mention 'authority' (1); Jesus gave them as His representatives something of the authority He had received from the Father. Luke alone mentions power as well. In both the Old and New Testaments miracles are recorded which were not from God, cf. Matt. **7**.22; **12**.27; **24**.24; Acts **8**.9; **19**.13; 2 Thess. **2**.9; Rev.**13**.13 f. Where these powers come from is unimportant, the authority behind them is what matters, and this authority is borne witness to by a Christ-like life. For further treatment of vs. 1–5 see comments on Luke **9**.51–**10**.16 in Study No. 35.

Jesus was 'the second man' (1 Cor. **15**.47), and neither then nor now do men take Him as He is. To identify Jesus with John the Baptist or Elijah (7 f) was an attempt to cut Him down to size and make Him easier to live with. We must always beware of explanations of Christ which have this effect.

Apart from the account of His death and resurrection the story of the feeding of the Five Thousand is the only incident told by all four evangelists. John **6**.6 makes it clear that the miracle was premeditated. Its effect (John **6**.15, 26) was precisely what He had foreseen in the first temptation (Luke **4**.3 f.). Since the long address in the Capernaum synagogue (John **6**.25–65) is not hinted at by the Synoptics, this cannot have been the primary purpose of the miracle. This may be hinted at in Mark **6**.52 (cf. Mark **8**.17–21). It was performed between the entrusting of authority to the Twelve on the one hand and the confession at Caesarea Philippi and the first foretelling of the passion (Matt. **16**.13–28) on the other. Before His humiliation of rejection and death they had to realize that Jesus was Lord not only of the storm-tossed sea and the individual but also of man's physical needs, not merely of his spiritual ones. It also brought home some of the implications of His passing on of His authority.

Note that more was left over than had originally been there (17). This rules out any theory of mass hypnosis. The modern idea that the boy's generosity (John **6**.9) shamed others into sharing what they had with them bears all the marks of modern sentimentality and accuses the evangelists of deliberate fraud.

Questions and themes for study and discussion on Studies 22-28

1. Jesus chose twelve disciples. Where else in the Bible do we find men being chosen to train for service under somebody else?
2. What is the relationship between doctrine and life?
3. Can we avoid all criticism from the world if we are faithful to God?
4. Why were not the mighty works done in the Galilean cities done also in Tyre and Sidon?
5. What may the preacher of the gospel learn from the parable of the sower?
6. Is there demon-possession today? If so, what are the marks of it?
7. Why do you think all the evangelists record the feeding of the Five Thousand?

SIX

The Galilean Ministry (3)

29 : Further Miracles

Matthew 15.21–39 (Mark 7.24–8.10)

Herod had been showing an unhealthy interest in Jesus (**14**.1 f.), and the Jerusalem religious authorities had challenged Him (**15**.1 f.), so He moved to areas outside their control (Mark **7**.24, 31). The NEB, Jer. B., and TEV are almost certainly correct in making the woman address Jesus as 'Sir' (22, 25); when she continued with 'Son of David', it is improbable that it meant anything special to her. Even if she was consciously calling Him Messiah, it was something she had picked up from Jews, who were plentiful in the area. Faith is not a blind cry in the night of need, nor is it the use of established formulae; there must be an element of understanding in it, and this she was given by verbal shock-treatment. First Jesus refused to react to a meaningless phrase (23). With v. 24 cf. Matt. **10**.6, Rom. **15**.8; if she had been sincere with her 'Son of David' she should have become a Jewess. Jesus' attitude brought her to her knees as a simple suppliant (25). In saying that it was not right to give the children's food to the house-dogs (26, Jer. B.) Jesus was not creating an either-or. The house-dog can expect to be fed, but cannot choose its food. The woman answered, 'I am asking only for some scraps' (27). Having come to see her position she received her desire. If there seems to be an element of hardness here, see Matt. **3**.9; John **8**.33, 39.

In the area north-east of the Sea of Galilee an unusually large crowd gathered, reminiscent of the early days in Capernaum (Mark **1**.32 f.), because Jesus had not been there before; it may have included many Gentiles. The testimony of the demoniac (Mark **5**.20) may have contributed. In the story of the five thousand we are told that it was out of compassion that He taught them and healed their sick (Matt. **14**.14; Mark **6**.34). Here (32) it is compassion for their hungry condition, especially as centres of supply were distant. So there is no reason to doubt that the miracle was performed primarily because of their physical need. No stress should be laid on the different words used for basket, in **14**.20 (*kopinos*) and in **15**.37 (*spyris*); the difference between them was in material and use rather than size.

30 : Peter's Confession

Matthew 16.13–28 (Mark 8.27–9.1; Luke 9.18–27)

Before they returned to Galilee Jesus challenged the Twelve to make up their minds about Him and then to face what the future was to bring. With the development of His ministry the first stirrings of Messianic hope seem to have died down, for He showed no desire to grasp political power; He was seen as a prophet, maybe Elijah come again as the forerunner of the Messiah (14). To the direct challenge, Peter said, 'You are the Messiah' (NEB), adding 'the Son of the living God', which in his mouth meant God's perfect revealer. In the light of John **1**.41 Jesus' reaction (17) may seem surprising. There is, however, a great difference between the confession of momentary enthusiasm, however commendable, and the expression of firmly based and intelligent conviction.

Were it not for the ecclesiastical claims built on it, no special attention would have been paid to vs. 18 f. They are not given in the other Synoptics, and v. 19 is balanced by **18**.18 and John **20**.23, in which the plural is used. More than the Twelve were present on the latter occasion, and the former presupposes far more than the apostles. The obvious interpretation of v. 18 is that the rock is Peter's confession. What we must not do is to find a pun on *petros* (Peter) = stone and *petra* = rock. The use of *petros* for a small stone was unknown in popular Greek. More important is that it was impossible in Aramaic (also Hebrew), which Jesus used. So the NEB translation is correct. Peter was rock so long as he stood on his confession. We need not deny him such priority as he clearly enjoys in Acts; it was limited and not transmittable.

Many moderns think of Jesus' death as a tragic accident caused by evil or undiscerning men. He foretold it, so that accident can certainly be ruled out, but only after the Twelve had realized who He was, lest they thought He had been crushed by the powers of the world. Jesus' obedience unto death demands a similar readiness from His disciples (24–27). Perhaps v. 28 means that relatively few of those present would experience the coming of His Kingdom. Mark **13**.32 has been held to rule out a reference to the second coming. An exclusive reference to the transfiguration, resurrection or coming of the Spirit would seem to be excluded by the time-factor, while the destruction of the Temple about forty years later misses the glory implied. It is perhaps best to understand that the whole opening period of the Church's history, culminating in the destruction of Jerusalem, is meant.

31: Transfiguration and Faith

Mark 9.2–29 (Matt. **17**.1–20; Luke **9**.28–43)

The transfiguration should be seen as the turning point in Jesus' ministry, even though this had been prepared for by the confession at Caesarea Philippi. Up to this point, in the obscurity of Nazareth and the publicity of ministry, Jesus had perfectly done God's will and had thus reached the goal Adam should have attained. Death had no claim on Him, and presumably He could have gone to the Father at once. The conversation about His departure (Luke **9**.31) marked His voluntary going on to the cross. Moses and Elijah (4) appeared as representatives of Old Testament revelation. The transfiguration probably took place on some high peak in Upper Galilee; neither Tabor nor Hermon suit the story. Ponder the discussion about Elijah's return (9–13) for the light it throws on some predictive prophecy.

In the story of the epileptic boy, it is important to identify the people referred to. The faithless generation (19) are primarily the disciples. We should not blame the father for his ' if you can ' (22), for the disciples had failed. ' All things are possible to him who believes ' (23) is not throwing the onus on the father but answering the ' if you can.' All things were possible to Jesus because He believed! The father misunderstood, but his cry with its very human self-contradiction (24) is only a parenthesis ignored by Matthew and Luke. It is in virtue of His own faith that Jesus cast out the spirit.

The disciples' question (28) was, in the light of Matt. **10**.1, entirely justified. The contrasting, but not contradictory, answers (29, Matt. **17**.20) show that Jesus' reply was longer than recorded. Matt. **17**.21 (AV) is a later adaptation; the addition 'and fasting' (29) is early but not original. The disciples as good Jews must have prayed before trying to cast out the demon, so it was not lack of prayer but wrong quality that was to blame. Prayer 'in the name of Jesus' involves a claim that we are acting as His representative. This is possible only if we are in living contact with Him through the Spirit and so know His will. Faith is the outcome of living fellowship with God. Behind much apparently confident prayer there is the attitude, 'Well, there's no harm trying.' 'If it be Thy will' is often a more honest expression of lack of faith. The one with true faith will, of course, not start praying contrary to God's nature.

32 : True Greatness

Mark 9.33–50 (Matt. **18**.1–9; Luke **9**.46–50)

The revealing of Jesus' Messiahship, the sense of growing tension and increase in popularity (Matt. **15**.30 f.), and the realization that three of their number had received some special privilege (**9**.2) made discussion on rank in the coming Kingdom a very human reaction (34). Jesus' answer should be read in conjunction with Mark **10**.35–45, where the issue is made even clearer; note the intensifying of 'servant' (35) to 'slave' (**10**.44). What part did the child play (36)? While we should take Matt. **18**.1–4 into consideration, this seems to refer to another case about the same time; indeed the whole section seems to be an outline of longer teaching. The great of the world normally recognize that a reputation for public service helps to maintain their position, i.e. they are serving for what they might get from it. Service given to a child has no reward to expect from the child. Jesus came not to be served but to serve (Mark **10**.45).

The relationship of this to John's words (38) is not obvious until we realize that he was objecting to the fact that 'he was not following US.' This unknown disciple was not detracting from Jesus' glory but from that of the twelve. The Church has always found it hard to come to terms with the Christian worker who ignores its book of rules. If even a cup of water given for Christ's sake has its reward, how much more the casting out of demons, even if carried out unorthodoxly.

The little ones (42) are firstly children, and then the child-like Christian (Matt. **18**.4). Many children have the door to discipleship closed for them by the contradiction between Christian profession and life, and the same has caused many converted persons to suffer from arrested spiritual development. We must take vs. 43–48 seriously, though not literally. The latter would imply that Christ's power is unable to bring the unruly member into subjection. The world clamours for self-expression; the Christian realizes that he is safe only as he limits that self-expression and, in the eyes of the world, maims his personality.

The commandment that salt should be offered with each sacrifice (Lev. **2**.13) was that it should be a reminder of the Covenant (Num. **18**.19). The addition in v. 49 (AV) comes from an early misunderstanding. The fire and salt is the removal of every sign of putrefaction.

33 : Free to do the Father's Will

John 7.1–14

Standing on the mountain top one may well catch glimpses of the road one followed to reach the summit. But many a surprise, many a hidden danger, many a possibility of going astray, awaits one before one reaches the foot of the mountain. The clearer the future and God's will seem to be, the readier we are to make plans, though in fact we have no real knowledge of what awaits us, and so often God reaches His purpose by means we could not have imagined. In this passage we are introduced to Jesus in a position where we might have supposed God's will to be clear. Challenged by His brothers to go to Jerusalem for the feast of Tabernacles, Jesus said He was not going. Behind the statement lay a two-fold meaning. One was that, if He went, it would not be for the motives they had indicated; the time for His arrest and execution, which had to take place in Jerusalem, had not yet come (6). Then, since God had not indicated any other reason for His going, He was staying away. Some days later (10)

God told Him to go, so He went. John's comment 'in private' merely underlines that He was not responding to His brothers' argument.

Such behaviour is so alien to us and to our way of thinking, that in comparatively early manuscripts v. 8 was changed to 'I am not going up yet', cf. AV. A well-meaning scribe thought he had to protect Jesus from the charge of lying. We find James rebuking some of his contemporaries for their light-hearted planning (4.13–16). Some promises about the future and some planning are unavoidable, especially in our more sophisticated and complex society. We should, however, always remember that, except where there is a clear indication of God's will, such planning can mean a limitation of God's right of control. We should particularly beware of commitments which effectively immobilize us until it is too late to respond. We cannot blame the world for creating such situations, though in its attempts to increase the mobility of labour it confesses its error, but the Church should not follow its bad example.

When Jesus arrived in Jerusalem, He found the Divine motivation for the delay. His absence had aroused far more comment than His presence could have. The result was that He had a far larger audience when He began to teach.

34 : The Water of Life

John 7.37–52

It is not certain whether by the last day of the feast (37) the seventh day of Tabernacles is meant, or the following day, which concluded the festival calendar (Lev. 23.36b). The weight of probability favours the former, but our understanding of Jesus' message will not be affected by our decision. Though the custom is not hinted at in the Old Testament, except possibly in Isa. 12.3, one of the chief features of Tabernacles in Jesus' day was the pouring out of water, brought from the pool of Siloam, at the foot of the altar during the morning sacrifice. It was both a thanksgiving that the water had lasted until then and a prayer that the early rains would soon fill their cisterns.

When Jesus spoke, this had been done for the last time that year. So, as with the Samaritan woman, and Jacob's well, He was clearly claiming to be the fulfilment of all that lay behind the water ceremony. As in Matt. **2**.23, no one Scripture passage lies behind v. 38; examples are Prov. **18**.4, Isa. **58**.11; Ezek. **47**.1–12. Perhaps the last fits the picture best, especially if we take it in the light of 1 Cor. **3**.16; **6**.19.

We find in vs. 40–43 perhaps the main reason why God countered Joseph's plan to bring up Jesus in Bethlehem. Not because Jesus was born in Bethlehem was He the Messiah, but because He was the Messiah He was born there, i.e. for the one who, on the basis of His life and teaching, accepted Him as Messiah, there was added as confirmation the fact that His birth had indeed fulfilled prophecy. A Jew may become convinced that all Messianic prophecies were fulfilled in Him, but that does not necessarily make him a Christian.

If the authorities had not ordered His arrest earlier (32), they would doubtless have done so after this claim. When the Temple police returned with empty hands, virtually spellbound by His words, they were rated for preferring a Galilean carpenter to the great men of Jerusalem (48). They discounted popular support and interest by the brutal words, 'As for this rabble, which cares nothing for the Law, a curse is on them' (49, NEB)—not ignorance but culpable ignorance was meant, but who would want to learn from these proud men? Nicodemus' protest was swept away by the illogical argument that prophets did not come from Galilee (52). In fact, Jonah was a Galilean, but even so, a prophet must be recognised by his message, not his birthplace.

Questions and themes for study and discussion on Studies 29-34

1. Ponder the fact that there must be an element of understanding in faith. Do we treat the teaching element in evangelism seriously enough?
2. Only Peter (or the disciples for whom he spoke) saw that Jesus was the Christ, the Son of God. Do the answers of the crowd show any insight at all?
3. Do you think the words 'listen to Him' (Mark **9**.7) would have had some special point for Peter in the light of Mark **8**?
4. 'A man often reveals his character when he gets a little power.' Consider this in the light of Mark **9**.35.

SEVEN

From Galilee to Jerusalem

35: Reactions to Jesus and His Message

Luke 9.51–10.16

The section **9**.51—**18**.14 is for the most part peculiar to Luke, and he has made no effort to fit it into Mark's framework. Indeed, to assume strict chronological order can lead to an exegetical nightmare. Much in these chapters cannot have taken place east of Jordan.

We may not assume that the Samaritan villagers knew of the events of John **4**.1–42. Their objection was to Jesus' going to worship in Jerusalem instead of at Mt. Gerizim (John **4**.20). Blindness and bigotry can be very annoying—is there any church where they are not found?—but that does not justify our calling down God's judgement on them.

The three men in vs. 57–62 are not types but individuals to whom Jesus speaks 'existentially', cf. **18**.18–23. Was the first (57 f.) afraid of hardship, or was he thinking like Peter (Matt. **19**.27)? Of the second (59 f.) we can be certain that though his father may have been on his death-bed, he was not dead. He was probably mainly concerned that the estate was fairly divided before he followed Jesus. If his father had been dead, the funeral would have been over in a matter of hours and Jesus would never have refused this act of filial piety. We cannot tell the background of the third (61 f.). His parents may have been miles away, or Jesus may have known that he would be unable to resist their entreaties.

With **10**.1–12, cf. **9**.1–6; Matt. **10**.1–15; Mark **6**.7–11; minor differences, e.g. no sandals (4), wearing sandals (Mark **6**.9) are easy to explain—it was a reserve pair that was being forbidden. Seventy-two (1, RSV mg., NEB) is almost certainly correct, i.e. six for each tribe. Though they were not missionaries, as we understand the term, but heralds and forerunners of the expected King, many missionary tragedies would have been avoided, if the principle of pairs, observed also by the Jerusalem church and Paul, had been followed.

The Jews claimed to be subjects of the King of heaven, the heathen to whom Paul went did not, hence Paul could not expect from them what Jesus' messengers had a right to expect in Jewish towns and villages. Similarly, the same drastic action (10 f.) would seldom be justified in a heathen environment, cf. Acts **18**.6.

36 : Rejection and Acceptance

Luke 13.22–35; 17.11–19

The question asked in v. 23 has been a common one at all periods of the Church's history; normally men have not hesitated to answer it according to their preconceptions. Jesus' refusal to answer—Matt. **7**.13 f. is a reference to His own time and situation—should check us. Does v. 29 really suggest only few? What is important is our personal reaction to it. Have I entered by the narrow door?

It is not easy to interpret vs. 31 f. On the whole, the fact that the Pharisees claimed to know Herod's plans and that they were told to carry a message to him suggests that they baulked at murder but would have been glad to see Jesus out of their area. In v. 32 we have a Hebraic idiom for a short time. Clearly, we cannot deduce from v. 33 that all prophets meeting a violent end died in Jerusalem, cf. 1 Kings **18**.4 and John the Baptist. Jesus meant that behind their death lay rejection by the spiritual leaders, who in His day were centred in Jerusalem. For the lament over Jerusalem see Matt. **23**.37–39, which probably gives the original setting, not reproduced by Luke. The same applies to v. 35, which looks to the second coming and not Palm Sunday (Luke **19**.38).

The rabbis interpreted Lev. **13**.46 to refer only to walled cities. In unwalled towns and villages the leper could live so long as no uninfected person shared his house. The boundary between Samaria and Galilee (**17**.11) was never clearly delineated, so there were mixed communities in which Jews and Samaritans doubtless kept well apart. A common fate had drawn the lepers together—the Samaritans kept the law of Moses, if anything, more strictly than the Jews. All ten showed faith; all ten were healed. Why did only one come back to say 'Thank you'? The experience of many a travelling preacher might suggest that there is nothing unusual in the proportion. Do you always thank the one through whom the power of God has been mediated to you? Note that the lack of gratitude did not mean the revocation of the healing. Yet lack of gratitude can involve lack of praise to God.

37 : Self-Forgetfulness and Self-Interest

John 11.54–12.11

Ephraim (54, 2 Sam. **13**.23) was an out-of-the-way place some fifteen miles north-east of Jerusalem. It served as a retreat for those avoiding authority, for, if followed, they could melt away into the wilderness. Note that Jesus used normal means to avoid His enemies, who had determined on His death (49 f.). Much in Holy Week becomes easier to understand when we grasp that the common people knew what the authorities intended (56). Those who lived at a distance from Jerusalem normally lived in a state of impurity until just before the great festivals. Some purification, cf. Num. **19**, could take a week, hence the early arrival.

These notes are perforce too brief to deal with the apparent chronological differences between the Synoptics and John with regard to Holy Week. It must suffice to say that if the triumphal entry into Jerusalem (**12**.12) took place on a Sunday, the arrival in Bethany must have been before sundown on the Friday and John has simply ignored the Sabbath, as would be quite natural for a Jew to do when recounting day to day events. In this case the meal would have been after the service, whether in the Temple or synagogue, that ushered in the Sabbath. At such a meal the women would eat after the men (2).

In fiction we should have been prepared for Judas' outburst and betrayal by indications of his state of mind. John was obviously shocked. Thinking back he will have seen pointers to what happened, but he spares us useless hindsight. How it was discovered that Judas was a thief we are not told. Probably his attitude and betrayal confirmed earlier vague suspicions. When he realized that his ambitions were not to be fulfilled through Jesus, he probably decided to save what he could from the wreck. 300 denarii (5) were nearly a year's wages, cf. Matt. **20**.2. In **11**.50 it was one man to die for the sake of the people; now two were threatened (10 f.).

EIGHT

Holy Week

38 : The Triumphal Entry

Matthew 21.1–11; John 12.12–19 (Mark **11**.1–11; Luke **19**.28–44)

We speak of Palm Sunday, but the only mention of palms is in John **12**.13, cf. Matt. **21**.8; Mark **11**.8. Palms do not grow readily round Jerusalem, and their thorns make them unsuited for a spontaneous demonstration. They had either been prepared in advance, or more probably were branches stored from the previous feast of Tabernacles (Lev. **23**.40). This was regarded as a Messianic feast (Zech. **14**.16), and Psa. **118**, as a Messianic psalm, was used during it. Hence the quotation of vs. 25 f. by the people. Hosanna is a popular corruption of *hoshia-na,* 'Save . . . we beseech Thee' (Psa. **118**.25). The most explicit form of the people's shout is in Mark **11**.9 f. Though a portion of the demonstration came from Jerusalem (John **12**.12), many there had no idea of what was happening (Matt. **21**.10 f.), and others joined in only later (John **12**.17 f.), when they knew that it was Jesus who was coming.

This all means that the Galilean pilgrims, both an earlier contingent already in Jerusalem and the main body with Jesus, had made a plot to place Jesus in such a compromising position with the Romans that He would be forced to declare Himself as Messiah. If He was to enter Jerusalem as planned, the only means of circumventing the plot was to seem to go with it, but to empty it of political seriousness by riding on an unbroken, frisky, donkey's colt—its mother was brought along (Matt. **21**.2) to keep it a little steadier. The way the donkey was fetched—its owner was doubtless one of Jesus' adherents—shows that Jesus knew that the pilgrims would have provided a more 'suitable' mount, had they known His plans. Though Jesus was fulfilling Zech. **9**.9, John **12**.16 makes it clear that neither the disciples nor the crowd realized this at the time.

If the question is asked why the Galileans did not call Jesus the Messiah clearly and openly, cf. Matt. **21**.11, the answer is probably that Jewish tradition considered this blasphemy until a person had shown his right to the title—the Romans doubtless understood the meaning of the terms used. If they did not react, it will be because Pilate had ample information about Jesus and as a result considered Him harmless. This comes out clearly in the subsequent trial.

39 : Empty Profession

Matthew 21.12–22 (Mark 11.11–25)

For the details of the cleansing of the Temple see the treatment of John **2**.13-16 in Study No. 12. Here no mention is made of a whip (John **2**.15). The prestige Jesus had acquired probably made His voice alone sufficient.

The order in Matthew and Mark is different. In the former the cleansing follows immediately after the Triumphal Entry, with the cursing of the fig tree on the next day; Mark puts both on the following day (Mark **11**.12). Since Matthew repeatedly ignores chronological order to stress spiritual connections, he has probably done so here also to show the King of Israel as Lord of the Temple. The story of the children (15 f.) is more likely to have happened before the priests were infuriated by the loss of their market. By His quotation of Psa. **8**.2 Jesus, by implication, accepted the Messianic dignity.

The mention of Jesus' hunger (18) shows that we have more than an acted parable. He was looking for the possibility of a few figs having been missed in the autumn gathering, which remained available to the passer-by. In the normal activities of life Jesus went by the same knowledge we all have. Not only were there no figs left, for which the tree was not necessarily to blame, but there was no trace of fruit to come; if there was to be any, it had to appear before the leaves. What followed had obviously a parabolic purpose. Since there is no evidence that the fig tree is used in the Bible as a picture of Israel, in spite of frequent affirmations to the contrary, the curse was a judgement purely on His own generation, which, in spite of its failure and the call to repentance, showed no sign of bearing worthy fruit. It is also a parable for every generation, Jewish or Gentile, where the same condition exists. Some conclusions about the poverty of His friends in Bethany may be drawn from the fact that Jesus was hungry so early in the morning.

Modern man is troubled as to why Jesus should have acted as He did; the Twelve were perplexed as to how His curse worked. Neither we nor they really grasped the lesson. This probably explains the apparently strange sequel in Mark **11**.24 f. Forgiveness is one of the main fruits God expects to find as a result of our repentance.

40 : The Problem of Authority

Matthew 21.23–46 (Mark 11.27–12.12; Luke 20.1–19)

We have dealt earlier with the question of authority under Mark **1**.21–42 and **2**.1–17 (Studies 35 and 36); it lay behind the repeated requests for signs (John **2**.18; **6**.30; Matt. **12**.38). Moses had authenticated his mission by signs (Exod. **4**.1–9, 29–31), so it was axiomatic to the religious leaders, as to Orthodox Jews today, that anyone coming, except as an expositor of Moses, would have to authenticate himself similarly. The weakness of signs is (*i*) that they may come from Satan (Matt. **24**.24; Rev. **13**.13–15; 2 Thess. **2**.9); (*ii*) normally grounds can be found for rejecting them. So Jesus challenged their willingness to accept through a case where no one suggested the activity of Satan—in spite of Matt. **11**.18—viz. John the Baptist. The importance of their response lay in their motivation. Had they sincerely been unable to come to an opinion, it would have shown spiritual obtuseness; their complete indifference indicated their unfitness to ask or judge.

In the parable of the two sons (28–32) the NEB and Phillips reverse the order of the sons, probably correctly, thus putting the one representing the chief priests and elders first. Some manuscripts give the answer 'The second' (31)—using the RSV order. As Schniewind says, this is so absurd and cynical that it is probably correct. We can picture a man like Caiaphas giving such an answer as a refusal to be heckled by a Galilean artisan. John's God-given ability to turn notorious sinners was sign enough. The same type of sign is valid also today, but just as the last word did not rest with John (John **3**.30), so it does not with the evangelist or teacher who is greatly used today.

The parable of the tenants (33–41) was addressed to the religious leaders of Israel, not to the people as a whole, who are represented by the vineyard (Isa. **5**.1–7). Hence v. 43 is no statement about the Jewish people as such; it is, in fact, applicable to spiritual leaders in the Christian realm who imagine that they have achieved a certain autonomy by virtue of their position, which enables them to judge what is best for the Church, whatever the Scriptures may say. God is sovereign, and those who believe they can exercise sovereignty on His behalf often end up by rejecting Him and so are rejected. There is no adequate reason for omitting v. 44, cf. margin and Luke **20**.18.

41 : The First Light of a New Day

John 12.20–50

The Greeks who wanted to see Jesus were Greek-speaking Gentiles of the type described in Acts as devout (**10**.2), worshippers of God (**16**.14), those that fear God (**13**.16); they attended the synagogue and kept the Noachic commandments (cf. Gen. **9**.1–7), i.e. they avoided practices that made social contacts with Jews impossible, but they had not become proselytes, i.e. full Jews. Their approach to Philip of Bethsaida (21) suggests they were from the Decapolis. Their coming to Jerusalem for the Passover showed real devoutness, for they were not allowed further than the Court of the Gentiles—had they been attracted by Jesus' clearing out of the market?—and they were not allowed to share in the Passover meal (Exod. **12**.48). A high proportion of the first Gentile Christians came from such circles.

John does not tell us the outcome of the request, though it is hard to believe it was refused; he is concerned that for Jesus it was the first ray of light at the end of the long 'valley of the shadow of death' He was entering He had to die, but by death far more life could come—Paul uses the picture of the corn of wheat in a slightly different way (1 Cor. **15**.36–38, 42–44). The way that Jesus went His disciples must follow (26).

The translation 'now is my soul troubled' (27) is somewhat misleading. In Hebraic thinking the soul is the whole man. With vs. 27 f. cf. the treatment of Matt. **26**.36–56 (Study No. 45). It is often suggested that Jesus shrank from death, partly because of the shame of the cross, partly from what was involved in His becoming sin (or a sin offering, cf. 2 Cor **5**.21). Heb. **5**.7 suggests that it was death itself that was the main load. To us who have 'to suffer the slings and arrows of outrageous fortune', who experience the decay of our bodies, who know that we *must* die, especially if we know we go to be with Christ, it is impossible to grasp what death meant to one who did not have to die. The lifting up (32, 34) was both crucifixion and exaltation.

In vs. 36b–41 we are introduced to a mystery of Divine activity, which receives fuller treatment in Rom. **9–11**. Though the New Testament never plays down the guilt of the Jewish authorities, and to a lesser extent of the Jewish people, here above all it is made clear they were co-operating in a purpose they did not know; they could not believe (39). We cannot acquit them for their rejection and we should not dare to judge them. The repeated and strange blindness shown by the Church is probably only another example of the same thing.

42 : Jesus Faces His Enemies

Luke 20.19–21.4; Mark 12.28–34 (Matt. 22.15–23.36)

All three questions put to Jesus (Luke **20**.21, 28; Mark **12**.28) were intended to drive a wedge between Him and sections of the people. That they might have further results was secondary.

(*a*) The question about tribute money was intended to alienate His Zealot supporters, who (if our interpretation in Study No. 38 has been correct) had been mainly responsible for the Triumphal Entry. One of their principles was that loyalty to God made it impossible to recognize any other power. A 'No' would have made Him a revolutionary in the eyes of the Romans.

(*b*) The concept of resurrection had become part of the faith of the common people (John **11**.24) largely because their conditions of life were so difficult. For Jesus to have been unable to defend it in the face of an obvious problem—the exaggerated question underlines the problem but does not create it—would have seriously discredited Him as a teacher. The question served as a swipe at the Pharisees as well.

(*c*) The scribe's question (Mark **12**.28) was more seriously meant, but he hoped to show that the establishment still stood above Jesus. In each case Jesus avoided the apparent dilemma by putting it in a different light or context. Whenever we facc such dilemmas we can be sure they exist only because we see them out of focus.

Jesus riposted immediately by showing that His opponents had become so immersed in matters of secondary importance, points of law and theology, that they were unable to answer vital questions (Luke **20**.41–44). In spite of the varieties of Messianic expression, each group expected Him to conform to their concepts instead of realizing that He was coming as Lord. Then Jesus told the people to have a second look at the establishment (45–47, the full attack is in Matt. **23**.1–36). An establishment, religious and civil alike, becomes inflated by its position. It is very rare for the best man to reach the top, specially if Mark **10**.43 is his ideal. So we must constantly turn from the position to the man and his behaviour. It was not so much that they were bad—the devouring of widows' houses may have been the result of perfectly legal claims secured by due process of law (47)—but they were acting a part, which did not express their inner nature—the meaning of hypocrite in the New Testament.

The story of the widow's mite (**21**.1–4) owes its position not merely to chronological order but because it stands in such contrast to the members of the establishment just mentioned. What little work she did we are not told, but she earned less than a fiftieth of the standard day's wage, and she gave the whole of it,

43 : The Last Supper

Matthew 26.20–35 (Mark **14**.17–31; Luke **22**.14–38; 1 Cor. **11**.23–26)

The Passover lamb was sacrificed on Nisan 14 and eaten on Nisan 15, which began at sunset. Since no leaven was left after midday on Nisan 14, the Gospels call it 'the first day of Unleavened Bread' (Mark **14**.12; Matt. **26**.17). Owing to the continual use of the words of institution, in later manuscripts the various accounts have influenced one another. The cup of Luke **22**.17 is the first cup of the Passover meal. There can be little doubt that the announcement of the betrayal (21–25) took place during the meal itself and that Judas left when it was finished—he could not have left before. To this day the meal is followed by an epilogue, begun by a distribution of unleavened bread. It was then that Jesus said, 'This is my body, which is for you' (1 Cor. **11**.24—'given' or 'broken' is not found in the earliest manuscripts). To end this section of the epilogue the Cup of Blessing (1 Cor. **10**.16) is drunk. Jesus gave it with the words, 'This is the blood of the covenant which is poured out for many.' The next section of the epilogue ends with the singing of Pss. **115–118** (30). After this the fourth cup should have been drunk; it was omitted, because, unlike the Passover, which looks back, the Lord's Supper looks forward to the Lord's Coming (Luke **22**.18; 1 Cor. **11**.26).

Looking at the earliest form of the words of institution, it appears as if the bread points to the Bread of Life and Jesus' perfect life rather than to His death, just as the unleavened bread looked forward to new life rather than the delivering sacrifice, pictured by the wine. Had theologians considered that near the beginning of the Passover ceremony the celebrant displays the unleavened bread saying, 'This is the bread of affliction that our fathers ate in the land of Egypt', many would have hesitated to read a mystic meaning into our Lord's words. 'For many' (28) links with Mark **10**.45, and this in turn with Isa. **53**.12, where 'many' is a Hebrew way of saying 'all, and they are many', cf. Rom. **5**.18 f. Jesus' linking of His death with the Passover celebration is the clearest evidence of the sacrificial nature of His death.

Just as Judas could allow Satan to enter him when he ignored Jesus' love (John **13**.27), so Paul warns those who participate in the Lord's Supper without due regard for that love (1 Cor. **11**.27–30). Equally, Peter's denial, in spite of Jesus' warning, shows that the Supper should speak to us of our weakness and need.

44 : Love and Betrayal

John 13

John depicts Jesus as the Passover lamb, dying on the cross at the time the lambs were being sacrificed (**19**.14–16). Therefore he does not present the Last Supper as a Passover meal (1). The explanation of the apparent contradiction must be that in that year for some reason the Passover was celebrated on two days. The Synoptics agree with the popular majority, John with that of the Sadducean establishment, but the ritual of the Passover shines through his narrative.

We are not told whether the disciples had washed their feet when they entered the Upper Room. Between the ceremonial tasting of the Passover symbols and the main meal there is a purely ritual hand-washing, cf. Mark **7**.1–8. Instead of a meaningless act, Jesus, taking the part of a slave, washed His disciples' feet, a task considered so menial as to be forbidden by the rabbis to a Jewish slave. His explanation was that, at such a feast, it could be presumed that all had bathed, but their feet would be bound to be dusty from the road (10), the application of which is found in 1 John **1**.6 f. It formed, too, a lesson in humble service. The literal interpretation of v. 14 found in some Christian circles would be rejected by Jesus as being as meaningless today as the ritual hand-washing He had ignored. We fulfil it by obeying the new commandment (34). It was the old one (1 John **2**.7–9; Lev. **19**.18), given an entirely new content by Jesus' example.

Many are puzzled by the disciples' inability to grasp Jesus' plain words to and about Judas (26–29, cf. Matt. **26**.25). There are acts of such evil malignity, committed even by Christians, that we do not want to believe them possible. The other disciples could conceive the possibility of betrayal in the abstract (Matt. **26**.22), but the reality stunned them. That Judas was satisfied with thirty pieces of silver shows that gain was not his main purpose. Was it that he had trusted completely that Jesus would fulfil his deepest longings for Israel, and that when he saw that he would be disappointed, his love turned to hatred? At any rate he became the dwelling place of Satan (27). The man who cannot face the reality of sin denies both the existence of Satan and that Judas became completely evil (Matt. **26**.24).

The religious Jew prolongs the Passover feast deep into

the night, so there is no difficulty in fitting John **13–17** into the Synoptic story.

45 : Gethsemane

Matthew 26.36–56 (Mark **14**.32–50; Luke **22**.39–53; John **18**.1–12)

Jesus made careful preparations that He should not be disturbed during the Last Supper by ensuring that Judas did not know where it would be held (Mark **14**.12–16). After the meal, however, He went and waited for the betrayal in Gethsemane, which Judas knew well (Luke **22**.39; John **18**.2). The traditional translation of Jesus' feelings is too tame. Much better is the NEB 'horror and dismay came over Him' (Mark **14**.33; Phillips, 'horror-stricken and desperately distressed'), 'My heart is ready to break with grief' (38, NEB). Even for Jesus the future did not become completely real until it was the present. Not until the load of human sin with which He was identifying Himself, was settling on Him, could the sinless One fully grasp its terrible nature. For a moment He felt lost, for the sinner is lost.

An adequate answer to the charge that Christianity involves determinism is given by Jesus' prayer (Mark **14**.36). There has to be man's willingness to accept. Phillips and the TEV get the sense better with, 'not what I want, but what You want'. Jesus does not say '*your* flesh' but 'the flesh' (41). Not the shrinking but the unwillingness to accept God's will is sin.

It may seem strange that Judas allowed so much time to elapse, for we must allow ample time for John **14–17**, the walk to Gethsemane and the period of prayer. The authorities had decided to postpone the arrest until after the feast (**26**.5); it was only Judas' news that Jesus knew He was to be betrayed and was apparently awaiting arrest that stirred them to action. All this meant delay. In addition Judas may have gone to the Upper Room first—the lanterns and torches (John **18**.3) would not have been necessary in Gethsemane under the full moon. The degree of malignity in Judas' betrayal is seen in his greeting, 'Hail, Rabbi', and the kiss (49). It was held that the pupil owed special loyalty to his teacher. There are varying renderings of v. 50. The NEB follows the

RSV mg., which the TEV expresses excellently, 'Be quick about it, friend!' Judas was accomplishing God's purpose for Him, so Jesus had no hard words for him. Note that non-resistance does not exclude protest against wrong (55 f.).

Those who today justify violence in a 'just cause' should never forget v. 52; it remains true.

46 : Jesus before Caiaphas

Matthew 26.57–75 (Mark **14**.53–72; Luke **22**.54–71; John **18**.13–27)

Today the view is often met that the trial story cannot be true because the behaviour of the Jewish court runs counter to the rules of procedure preserved in the Talmud. These are Pharisaic rules, demonstrably drawn up at a later date; at the time of Jesus justice was in Sadducean hands, and since the Pharisees considered them far too harsh, we need not doubt the truth of the judicial process described. The questioning before Annas (John **18**.13, 19–24) was informal; Caiaphas was not yet available, for he was probably arranging next morning's trial with Pilate.

The witnesses were false (59) in the sense that they tried to present Jesus' words and acts in a false light; liars would have agreed. The one serious accusation was a twisted form of what Jesus had really said (61, John **2**.19) but it was insufficient to justify a death sentence. Caiaphas' adjuration, 'In the name of the living God, I now put you on oath: tell us if you are the Messiah, the Son of God' (63, TEV), was contrary to every form of natural justice. In His answer (64) Jesus identified Himself with the Son of Man of Dan. **7**.13, the coming ruler of the world, not only at the end of time but 'from now on' (NEB, Jer.B., TEV). Since Caiaphas could hardly have understood 'Son of God' in the Christian sense, the blasphemy was presumably the claim to be the Messiah before having demonstrated by actions His right to the title.

The Sanhedrin being far from complete at its night meeting, owing to its having been so hurriedly convened, its decision was confirmed at a fuller meeting at dawn (Luke **22**.66–71).

It is usually assumed that John was the disciple who

enabled Peter to enter Caiaphas' palace (John **18**.15 f.). Probably the maid at the door had no malice behind her statement (69), but it made Peter feel suddenly that he had entered the lion's den. Once having denied it was hard to confess. The translations of v. 74 and Mark **14**.71 may well be too charitable to Peter; it was probably on Jesus that Peter was calling down the curses as proof positive. The mention of the double cock-crow in Mark **14**.30, 72, as against the single one in the other Gospels, goes back to Peter himself.

47 : The Crucifixion

John 19.1–37 (Matt. **27**.24–50; Mark **15**.15–37; Luke **23**.24–46)

Pilate's position, in one way, was like Peter's. He was not obliged to try Jesus; once he decided to he had sufficient secret service information to discharge Him at once, but once he hesitated he was lost. In vs. 1–16 we have his last despairing, unavailing attempts to extricate himself. The Jewish authorities too were carried away by the tide; they had never expected to acknowledge Caesar as king (15). 'The Jews', as so often in John, are the religious leaders. The only role the people played centred in Barabbas (Mark **15**.6–15). The fiery nationalists felt that Jesus had let them down; if they had to choose between Him and Barabbas, they considered the latter had more to offer them. The contrast often drawn between the Triumphal Entry and 'Crucify!' is often ill-conceived. They had hailed Him then not for what He was but for what they thought Him to be.

John, writing after the Synoptics, and so leaving other details to them, confines himself to a picture of the King, all hesitation past, going serenely to His throne on the cross. Three times we find Scripture mentioned as being fulfilled. The soldiers blindly carried out Psa. **22**.18 (24). Note that though the Synoptics mention the division, they do not link it with the psalm. It was not invented, as the sceptic maintains, to provide a fulfilment. Then Jesus deliberately provided a fulfilment of Scripture in quoting Psa. **69**.21, thereby linking Himself with all who suffer for righteousness' sake. Finally, God overruled the disposal of His body, that He might be seen to be the true Passover lamb (36). This looks forward to the fulfilment of Zech. **12**.10, cf. Rev. **1**.7.

John stresses that out of Jesus' spear-pierced side came blood and water, cf. 1 John **5**.6. Medically, the meaning is disputed. Spiritually, we can be certain that John was meeting the view of many contemporaries that Jesus did not really die and was not fully man. Then, too, though 'the blood of Jesus Christ' means His death, John saw His blood poured out like that of the sacrificial animals. The water speaks of His purifying power. As Toplady wrote:

Let the water and the blood,
From Thy riven side which flowed,
Be of sin the double cure—
Cleanse me from its guilt and pow'r.

Questions and themes for study and discussion on Studies 38-47

1. From the time of Peter's confession at Caesarea Philippi Jesus sought to show His disciples what *kind* of Messiah He had come to be. How would the events of Palm Sunday help this educative process?
2. The Temple was twice cleansed, but why has God given us a record of both occasions?
3. Can we tell whether a miracle is from God or Satan?
4. What anticipations of the extension of the gospel to the Gentiles do we find in the ministry of Jesus?
5. Study the wisdom of Jesus on the Day of Questions.
6. Why do you think Jesus instituted the Lord's Supper?
7. What place is there for symbolic acts in the life of the Christian?
8. Was the experience in Gethsemane necessary? Does it make His sacrifice at Calvary even more meaningful?
9. How could a religious leader employ liars and reject the very Son of God?
10. Why is John especially emphatic about the water and the blood?

NINE

The Resurrection and Ascension

48 : The First at the Tomb

John 20.1–23 (Matt. **28**.1–10; Mark **16**.1–8; Luke **24**.1–12)

It is comparatively easy to weave the four narratives of Jesus' trial and death into one, but this is really impossible with the resurrection story. It is as though the apostles took great care that the narrative of their Lord's death should raise no questions by seeming contradictions. With the resurrection, however, the shout is, 'We have seen Him; He is alive for evermore!', and so the individuality of personal experience receives its full expression.

The use of 'we' (2) shows that there is no conflict with Matt. **28**.1; Mark **16**.1. In all versions of the story great stress is laid on the stone. This is usually pictured as one in the shape of a wheel, moving in a groove. The use of such stones was rarer than generally assumed, and the language fits a boulder moved into position at least as well, cf. Matt. **28**.2; with such a stone the anxiety of the women is easy to understand. What Peter and John saw was the grave-cloths, long linen strips, still maintaining, thanks to the spices, the shape of the body, and the cloth that had been around His head, where it had rested. The resurrection body of Jesus had passed out of the burial cloths and tomb. The stone had been rolled away that men might see the tomb was empty; the cloths had been guarded by the angel (Matt. **28**.5) that the two disciples might see them untouched and so believe (8). The comment in v. 9 means that they should have believed, but did not, on the basis of the Old Testament alone.

To each according to his need: for John the grave-cloths sufficed, for heart-broken Mary the personal revelation, for Peter a meeting so intimate that no more than its fact is told (1 Cor. **15**.5; Luke **24**.34). Let us never try to force our relationship with the living Lord into a fixed pattern. Jesus would never have denied Mary (17) what He offered Thomas (27), so the AV is badly at fault; the RSV 'hold' is adequate, but the best is 'Do not cling to me' (NEB, Jer. B.).

Jesus prepared the ones He loved most carefully (by His earlier appearances) for His first group appearance. There were more than the Eleven present (Luke **24**.33, 36), a fact of importance for our understanding of vs. 22 f. If Jesus' eating (Luke **24**.41 f.) was a mark of loving condescension, it is reasonable to think that the marks of the nails and spear were equally so, the more so as the other marks of the passion are not mentioned. Doubtless those who would feel that something were missing in heaven without them will see them there also.

49 : The Road to Emmaus

Luke 24.13–43

Though the story of Jesus' joining a pair of dispirited disciples on their way home to Emmaus is a favourite one, we seldom ask ourselves why this otherwise unknown pair—was the unnamed one Cleopas' wife?—was granted a privilege apparently given to no others. If, as seems probable, they lived in Emmaus, they belonged to the relatively small number of Judeans who had put their trust in Jesus. They had not been able to hear His Galilean teaching, and though they lived only seven miles from Jerusalem, they could easily miss much that was happening there. As said before, 'To each according to his need'.

There is here an interesting repetition. Not merely to the two on the road (27) but also to the larger company in the upper room (44–47) Jesus went through the Old Testament, explaining the prophetic statements about Himself. This is recorded by Luke as a claim that the Christian treatment of the Old Testament, often strange to the Jew and foolish to the modern expositor, was in fact derived from Jesus Himself. To say this is not to justify the forcing of Old Testament texts to bear an impossible Messianic meaning, which is still often met. If we look at the New Testament evidence more closely, we shall see that its writers are normally more concerned with Old Testament *passages* than individual texts; when these are quoted they often point to their context as a whole.

We are assured here that Jesus' resurrection body was a real one (39). It is highly improbable that the non-mention of blood is significant. At the same time the body was under the influence of spirit in a way we can only dimly understand. The concept of 'psychosomatic' has become a commonplace in modern medicine, both for sickness and health, but those using it do not know how it works. We are not granted the powers of physical transformation possessed by our Lord, but we do have the spirit transforming us from glory to glory (2 Cor. **3**.17 f.). This does not mean that we should be free from illness and physical weakness, as some maintain, but that, when they come, they can be welcomed as God's will.

'While they still disbelieved for joy' (41); this is an element for which we do not always allow. The gospel is so wonderful, that some on hearing it genuinely fear disappointment, especially when they see Christian lives falling short of it,

50 : My Lord and my God

John 20.24–31

Thomas was one of those who disbelieved for joy. A natural pessimist, he was absolutely devoted to Jesus (**11**.16). It may well have been the depth of his sorrow that kept him from the fellowship of his companions (24). The very vehemence of his words—'I refuse to believe' (Jer. B.) gives the sense better—betrays his desire to be convinced. Once again we have an example of 'To each according to his need.' It is highly improbable that he availed himself of Jesus' invitation, but the graciousness and super-human knowledge displayed by Jesus swept him to his knees with the glad cry, 'My Lord and my God.'

Thomas was a devout Jew for whom the existence of only one God was axiomatic. Had he been challenged to justify his words intellectually, he could not have done so, but he would not have retracted them. The belief in the deity of Jesus Christ and the resultant doctrine of the Trinity are not the fruit of some theoretical theology, but the only possible expression of our experience of His saving and transforming power. This should always be remembered, when we speak to Jews, Muslims, some heretical sectarians and atheists. We preach a crucified and risen Christ. If they come to know Him, the rest will follow also.

It is not only in New Testament times that man has experienced 'To each according to his need'. Today also many are tempted to feel despondent, when they hear ecstatic testimonies to marvellous experiences of Divine grace, with whatever label they may be named. It is then that we should remember 'Blessed are those who have not seen and yet believe'. Very often those who receive such outstanding signs of Divine love are babes who cannot walk by faith but need sight. It is Divine love that enables many to walk without sight, and blessed are they.

Just as the evangelists left much unrecorded (30), so these comments have passed over much in silence, and for the same reason. Anything that does not create deeper faith that Jesus is the Messiah, God's King, and lead to discipleship has little value for the normal Christian, however true it may be, and however much it may be useful to the Christian apologist.

51 : The Ascension

Matthew 28.16–20; Luke 24.44–53

Ever since Jesus Christ ascended to heaven the Church has been demonstrating His power by its walk of faith. To a very few He has, for a brief moment, vouchsafed a fleeting vision of Himself, but for the rest the Christian walk has been by means of the unseen and often unfelt influence of the Holy Spirit making Him and His will real. Under the influence of the modern demythologizer the story of the Ascension is scorned, but so long as man remains within the space-time continuum, which conditions our experiences of nature, there was no other way in which it could be made clear to His disciples and to us, that Jesus Christ had passed with His perfect manhood and resurrection body to a mode of existence of which we know nothing, there to rule until every enemy is put under His feet.

The story in Matt. **28**.16–20 is probably that referred to in 1 Cor. **15**.6. The Eleven will not have been among the doubters, but only they are mentioned to make it clear that Jesus' command was one to the Church, which is built on their teaching (Eph. **2**.20). There are rare cases where someone must go out completely alone, but normally there should be co-operation between church and individual, cf. Acts **13**.1–3. We cannot claim the promise of Christ's presence (20) unless we are where He wants us to be.

We always long to make a completely new beginning, to cut off the disastrous past, but not so God. Jerusalem and its temple were already under the sentence of destruction (Luke **19**.41–44), but it had to be from there that the gospel went out first. Today also, unless we are prepared to make the gospel credible where we are called (1 Cor. **7**.24), we are not likely to make it so where we are unknown.

One feature of the Primitive Church is its apparent lack of urgency—urgency and intensity are different matters. The initial command to wait (Luke **24**.49) was realized to be more than a mere waiting for the Holy Spirit. Acts is full of stories showing how God opened new doors when the time was ripe. Equally, the Son of God waited thirty years in Nazareth being prepared. When God has taught us the lessons we have to learn, He will move us without delay.

Questions and themes for study and discussion on Studies 48-51

1. The disciples saw the actual moment of the ascension. Does it matter that they did not see the actual moment of the resurrection?
2. What Old Testament passages do you think would have figured in that wonderful discourse on the road to Emmaus?
3. If we have not seen and yet believe, is our faith blind or does it have some basis of knowledge other than physical sight?
4. Does the Great Commission still apply?